FIVE YEARS IN INDIA

Comprising

A Narrative of Travels in the Presidency of Bengal,
A visit to the Court of Runjeet Singh,
Residence in the Himalayah Mountains, an account of
The Late Expedition to Cabul and Afghanistan,
Voyage down the Indus,
and Journey Overland to England

by

Henry Edward Fane, Esq
Late Aide-de-camp to his Excellency the Commander-in-Ghief
in India

IN TWO VOLUMES

VOL. I

Nirmal Publishers & Distributors

B-2, Vishal Enclave, New Delhi - 110027

Published by
NIRMAL PUBLISHERS AND DISTRIBUTORS
B–2, Vishal Enclave, New Delhi-110027
Phone : 5413460

Reprint : October 1986

PRICE : Rs. 125-00

Printed at :
Anubhav Art Press
Raghubir Nagar, New Delhi-110027

CONTENTS

TO

THE FIRST VOLUME

CHAPTER I.

CHAPTER II.

Page

CHAPTER IX.

CHAPTER X.

Page

CHAPTER XI.

CHAPTER XII.

CHAPTER XIII.

CHAPTER XIV.

CHAPTER XV.

CHAPTER XVI.

Five Years in the East.

CHAPTER I.

Ordered for Foreign Service—Embarkation—Vile Climate of Cork—Ship aground—Return to Plymouth—Desertion—Re-embarkation—Discomforts of a Sea-voyage—A Novel Remedy for Sea-sickness—Off Madeira—A Man Overboard—Amusements at Sea—Crossing the Line—Albatross—Tristan d'Acunha—A Soldier's Funeral at Sea—Short of Provisions.

In June or July, 1835, a report first began to spread among us that our regiment, to whose turn it had nearly come for foreign service, was to be sent to Ceylon ; which, though at first disbelieved, was soon found to be but too true : for in the course of a few weeks we found ourselves at Cork, there to await the transports destined for our embarkation.

After much delay from the foul weather our ship had in coming round, early in October she did at last make her appearance ; and on the 20th, the head-quarters and nineteen officers of the regiment (the 90th), among whom I ranked, embarked in her at Cove.

Few of us, I believe, much regretted leaving Cork ; for in spite of its beautiful scenery and pleasant society it was, during the time we remained there, blessed with such a climate as I have never been in either before or since. It rained or snowed almost every day, and when it did happen to do neither of these, our barracks, being placed on the top of a huge hill, gave us the benefit of every wind that blew ; which were *not* "few or far between."

For several weeks after embarkation contrary winds prevented our getting out of the Cove of Cork, which, in the middle of winter and in a crowded ship, were serious *desagremens*. At last, to complete our misfortunes, our ship ran aground, and though found not to be materially damaged, still that having sprung a leak it would be necessary to go to Plymouth to refit. Accordingly, on the first change of wind, instead of starting for the East, we sailed for Plymouth, in which beautiful harbour we anchored on the third day.

After some little discussion it was found necessary to disembark the troops ; which was accordingly done, and myself and a brother officer, with a detachment, took up our quarters in Mount Wise with a depot of the 98th regiment, whose kindness and excellent mess I shall long remember.

The cold and discomfort of ship-board seemed to please our men as little as their officers, and though on our first embarkation we had not lost a man, and all seemed cheerful at the thoughts of foreign service, yet, after the experience they had already had, we found that many declined a second trial ; and though some were again brought back, still our muster-rolls at our second embarkation on the 4th of January wanted several of their usual complement, from desertion.

Poor fellows ! one could not blame them, for nothing could be worse than the arrangements made for their comfort and convenience by the Transport Board. Instead of their deck being fitted with hammocks, which could be taken down during the day, and thus leave space for the free circulation of air, the place had been blocked up with what are termed berths, or standing bed places ; which made it far more difficult to keep the place clean, and contributed neither to the comfort nor convenience of its occupants.

The officers, portion of the main deck was scarcely more comfortable, seventeen of us being crowded together in a portion of the steerage, in wooden berths ranged one above another ; and all the duties of the toilet had to be performed in the passage between the lines of berths, up and down which people were continually passing. Our passage, as far as the ship went, was found for us ; but, contrary to the usual practice of a mess being found for officers by government, we had to pay at the rate of ten shillings per day, which formed at the end of the voyage a bill about equivalent to a year's pay.

But to return to our voyage. We sailed at last, finally, on the 9th of January, 1836, with a contrary wind blowing hard from the S.S.W. But having positive orders from the Admiral to sail, wind fair or foul, go we must ; and after a time the wind having come round some points, by night we managed to make a good offing.

Our ship, the Sir Charles Malcolme, a large Bombay Indiaman of 960 tons, proved a stout and safe, though slow ship, built entirely of teak, and well formed to battle with the hurricanes of the China seas ; for which trade she had been originally intended.

As usual with young sailors, almost every one save our Colonel, and one or two others, were as sick as men could well be ; against which, however, I believe the Colonel gave us the best antidote, by obliging us to keep watch strictly, and forbidding the officer in charge to go down until he had seen his successor on deck ; who, of course, took care to make the unfortunate wretch come, sick or not, by pulling him out of bed, or some such gentle means.

I am quite sure that, in the end, this was the best remedy for sea-sickness that could have been chosen ; and often as I have been with parties on ship-board since, I never saw any set who got over that most miserable of all misfortunes quicker than we did in this instance. Some few began to make their appearance the second day, and on the third all put a bold face on the matter. But that bugbear to all Cockney travellers, the Bay of Biscay, sent the ladies down again ; and even some of the men began to look uncomfortable. But it did not last long, and by the time we approached Madeira all was well.

On the 24th of January we made the island of Madeira, at which we fondly hoped we were to touch ; but from some shift in the wind, or in our captain's mind, we were doomed not to land and by night we had left this beautiful island far behind.

Porto Santo, the island we first made before seeing Madeira, seems but a barren rock, through I believe it is inhabited. Of Madeira we could see but little, save a distant view of its woods, and vineyards, and high rocky coast.

Jan. 25th.—Exchanged colours with the Fergus of Liverpool—an event at sea. All glasses up to see what species of animals the parties bound for Calcutta in this ship might be, and on whom many sage conjectures were of course made.

As a journal at sea usually contains little more than a repetition of "shoal of porpoises in sight"—"Bonito round the ship," and other remarks of a like novel and important nature, one may safely leave out all such matters without any loss to the world at large.

February 2nd. Lat. 13° 32′—Was aroused about seven from a comfortable nap, by the cry of "A man overboard!" Slipped my clothes on, and ran upon deck, in time to see them lower the starboard cutter, and proceed in pursuit of him. He turned out to be a Lascar, half an idiot, but, luckily for him, an excellent swimmer; so that in ten minutes he was picked up, much exhausted, and brought back. Nothing can be more awful than this cry of "A man overboard!" it arouses every one, from the lowest to the highest, in the ship, and the state of anxiety of all is indescribable. To us no such misfortune happened as losing a man in this manner, but since then it has occurred to me; and till experienced, few can believe how universal is the gloom such an event produces on all.

Among other ship amusements started for the pastime of all parties was an amateur theatrical performance, the first of which took place near the line on the 6th; and, considering all things, it was a very creditable affair. A newspaper also was published on board, doing great credit to its editor, and giving infinite amusement to all of us.

February 9th. Lat. 1° 12′ N.—Joined a brig, for some time supposed to be outward bound, and the first cutter was lowered down; when a crew composed of our own and the ship's officers boarded her. What with straw hats and red nightcaps, we at first took them for pirates; but she turned out to be the Countess of Airlie, bound for Monte Video, and our letters must consequently wait a better opportunity.

February 10th. Lat. 0° 40′ N.—Nothing particular occurred during this morning, except the catching of a small shark. But towards evening symptoms of the usual ceremonies on passing the line began to appear, and we were all well ducked, preparatory to being shaved the following day.

February 11th.—Neptune's visit has been too often described by better authors than myself; I shall therefore only say that this morning was enacted that greatest of all farces, Neptune's visit, in which we were ducked, shaved, and made uncomfortable for the next week. Strange to say, some were pleased with this; but to my taste it was both *frivolous, and vexatious* and without meaning; and I being bored by it and making some opposition, was, perhaps deservedly, treated with an extra dose.

February 12*th.*—Rose with a headach from the effects of yesterday's paint. Bestowed my maledictions on the authors thereof, and walked on deck in time to see the catching of a small shark by one of the ship's officers. Spoke to and boarded the William of Rotterdam, by which the despatches and our own private letters were sent home.

February 13*th.* Lat. 1° 6′.—Spoke to and boarded another brig, called the Congo of Bristol, from Bony, on the west coast of Africa, laden with palm-oil.

March 8*th*.—On nearing the Cape, the sameness of ship-board is somewhat relieved by the flocks of albatross, Cape pigeon, and other birds which surround the ship; and of these we had numbers. Many of the first were caught and brought upon deck; some of them measured nine feet from wing to wing. Those we caught were of the white kind, and were very fine birds. We tried to take some of them with us to Ceylon, but found after a time that they merely pined away, and the attempt was consequently given up in despair.

March 10*th.*—Made and passed the island of Tristan d'Acunha, at about forty miles distant, and of which but one high peak was visible, which is said to be 9000 feet above the level of the sea.

On the 15th we had our first funeral of a grown-up person at sea, in that of a solider of our regiment. I know nothing more impressive than a military funeral at all times; but it is particularly so at sea, when, as in this instance, the winds and the waters are high, and the solemn music of the band can only be heard at intervals rising above the sounds of the tempest : its impressiveness in doubly felt.

From the 21st to the 24th inclusive we were rounding the Cape, amidst very heavy and disagreeable weather, carrying away sundry spars, and frightening the women out of their wits. We, however, worked through without much difficulty ; though not without experiencing that mighty sea to the full, which I believe almost always runs on L'Agulla's bank, and which causes the loss of many a good ship in the course of every year.

After getting safely and well into 9° 16′ S. lat., and longitude 64° 56′ E., it was found that, from the shortness of provisions, we should be obliged to change our course, and steer for the Seychelles, a group of islands to the north of Madagascar, where we knew all our wants could be supplied. To some this proved a nuisance, but for myself I cared little about it, and on the contrary thought that, while one was about it, one might as well see these islands as be boxed up in the island of Ceylon, which at that time I expected would be my home for many a-day.

CHAPTER II.

Harbour of Mahe—Importance of Fortifying it—Anchor in Colombo Roads—First Impressions of Ceylon—Colombo—Society in Ceylon—Change of Places—The Author appointed to the Staff of Sir Henry Fane—Visit to the Governor—Botanic Gardens—Extraordinary Excavation—Disembark at Madras—Splendid Living there—Re-embark on board the Asia, for Calcutta—Departure from Ceylon—Becalmed—Arrival at Calcutta—Life in the City of Palaces—A State Dinner—Trip up the Country—Religious Prejudices of the Natives—Barackpore—Behrampore—Splendid New Palace—Patna—Company's Opium Factory—Dinapoor—Horse-breeding Establishment at Buxar—Tomb of Lord Cornwallis—Arrival at Benares.

At length, our good ship cast anchor in the harbour of Mohe, the principal harbour and port of this group of islands; and for the first time I beheld the tropical land, and a more beautiful specimen could not be. The mountains rise abruptly from the water to the height of 1500 feet, covered with the most luxuriant growth of Oriental timber, underneath which the pine-apple grows wild in all directions, which, when we landed, was nearly ripe. The language spoken is entirely French, and, with the exception of the Governor and our detachment of the 99th regiment, stationed as garrison on the island, few could speak English.

After four months on ship-board, the verdure and beauty of these islands were most refreshing, and the few days we spent there were employed by most of us in scrambling over the rocks, shooting, and stuffing cocoa-nuts, pine-apples, and any trash we could get hold of—the luxury of any thing green, either in fruit or vegetables, being only to be appreciated by those who have been for months at sea.

The principal islands of this archipelago were explored in 1743, by Lazarus Picault, and named after Mahe de la Bourdonnais, than Governor of the Mauritius. They are situated in a great bank of soundings, Mahe being the largest, which is about sixteen miles long and five broad, in which is the harbour, where we anchored, off Batt River. It is inhabited by from 60 to 100 white families, who once had a considerable trade in cocoa-nut oil, collecting tortoise-shell, and building small vessels. But of late years this trade has been much diminished, in consequence of the emancipation of their slaves and the departure of many of the French settlers.

This fine harbour of Mahe is without fortifications, but might be very easily defended, from its precipitous hills and deep ravines ; nor could ships of war come near enough the town to fire effectually upon it without entering the inner harbour, which is narrow and very intricate. Its situation would render it a very important place in the hands of an enemy, who might easily make it a superb shelter for their privateers, employed in the interruption of our trade.

This place is celebrated for its shells, of which numbers were brought for our inspection. The sea here was more beautifully clear than in any place I ever was in, the coral reefs being to be seen at all times, though far below the surface. Numbers of a bad kind of turtle are also to be seen here at times.

Wednesday, the 4th of May, we weighed anchor, and stood out of the harbour, passing the island of St. Ann's, and several others ; and from thence we stood fairly away for Ceylon, having received all the necessary supplies on board. On the 20th, we passed in sight of Cape Comorin, the southernmost point of the great continent of India, and on the 22d anchored in Colombo

Roads, and soon after received orders to disembark the following morning.

In the evening, many of the civil and military officers stationed at Colombo came off to hear the news, and at the same time to give some to us. Each and all spoke favourably of the climate, though their appearance rather told a different tale. Our ship was too large to go over the bar—a reef of rocks about half a mile from the shore, over which the surf runs very high ; and she was consequently anchored some little distance out at sea, which made the disembarkation somewhat more difficult and dangerous.

All our party were, I think, much disappointed with the first appearance of Ceylon, which, in one's mind's eye, had appeared a mountainous and superbly wooded country ; in place of which we saw a low sandy beach, on which the surf was beating high, backed by cocoa-nut trees down to the water's edge, among which appeared the white houses of the residents.

In the evening, we all dined at the excellent mess of the 58th regiment, as honorary members of which we remained until the formation of our own. What we see of the town of Colombo we like much : the streets are wide, with double rows of trees down the centre. It is kept very clean, and the painted verandahs and house-fronts give it, altogether, rather a cheerful look.

The fort in which we all resided, and which is in fact the European town, is situated between the sea and a large fresh-water lake, joined to the main by a narrow strip of land. The works in it are mostly old Ducth ones, and quite as strong as we are ever likely to require there.

There is but little amusement round the town in the shooting way, the cinamon gardens, which run for ten miles in every direction, affording but little shelter for game. The heat at this time we all voted enormous, but I afterwards found to my cost that it was nothing to that of the continent of India. The beautiful lake behind the fort both looks and is the coolest place around ; and accordingly several of us set about establishing boats. Many of the principal residents have houses on its banks, and among others Sir T. Wilson, the Commander-in-chief of the troops. Most of the residents who are permitted to do so live at Calpetty, a suburb on the sea-side, and the houses built here are borh the coolest and best at Colombo. They are most of them of one story, with long low verandahs stretching along their whole length with large rooms, through which care is taken to preserve a thorough draft.

Our time, after we landed, was pretty much taken up by a succession of parties, balls, and picnics ; and these, with arranging one's household, took up the greater part of it. I got, with a brother officer, one of the many small bungalows in the fort, and had just begun to get settled and comfortable when I received my appointment to the staff of my uncle, General Sir Henry Fane, the then Commander-in-chief in India. This, of course, altered all my plans, and I again began making my preparations for sea, and for quitting the island.

On the 29th of June, I went on board a small brig, the Warwick of Liverpool, whose accommodation I found to be good enough for my short voyage, and accordingly secured a berth on board her. In the mean time the Governor having kindly asked me to pay him a visit at his country.house at Candy, I determined not to miss so good an opportunity of seeing a small part of the interior ; accordingly, on the 6th, I left Colombo at gunfire, by what is here called the mail, a species of double-bodied phaeton, drawn by two horses, and holding there passengers and the coachman. Though an English Jehu might smile at this turn-out, still it answers every purpose required of it, and is, moreover, a very great convenience to travellers between the two capitals.

Nothing can be more perfect than the road on which we travelled, or more beautiful than the scenery on either side as you advance. It was cut by Sir E. Barns, and cost a very large sum of money ; which is, however, admirably laid out. The timber in many parts is very fine, particularly in the Kadijinawa Pass—a noble effort of engineering, about twenty miles from Candy.

Our coach arrived in time to allow us to meet a large party at Sir W. Horton's table, who each day gave me a mount, and enabled me to see as much of the environs of Candy as my limited time would permit. The chief lions are the beautiful neighbourhood ; the Botanical Gardens, kept up at the expense of government ; and an extraordinary excavation through a neighbouring mountain, the object of which it is difficult to conceive. I had not sufficient time to see this fine country properly, as my ship was daily expected to sail. The Government house at Candy is a very fine specimen of the style of houses built for European occupation : large and airy, the walls covered with a composition called chunam, which bears a polish almost equal to marble, and has the best possible effect.

The old palace of the Candian princes is a large and curious specimen of native architecture, now converted into government offices, store-houses, &c., while the last king is banished to India. In point of climate, Candy is very superior to its rival capital, and I should say in every way superior.

On the 9th, I again left Candy, reached Colombo in safety, and spent the three following days in preparing for my voyage, and bidding a long farewell to my old regiment and other friends.

At length, on the 14th, I embarked in the Warwick for Madras, with a heavy sea running, which made it somewhat difficult to get on board. It was, however, accomplished, and we stood away from Ceylon, passing along the island some thirty miles distant.

July 18th.—Latitude 6° 36′.—We have passed, during the night, the southern part of Ceylon, and are now coasting the eastern side of the island, which appears much the same kind of coast as that of Colombo. We shall probaly pass Trincomalee during the night, and get fairly into the bay of Bengal. A strong monsoon, with fine, though hot weather.

July 25th—Blowing very heavy during the greater part of the night from the land, which sent us many miles to leeward of our course, under double-reefed topsails, accompanied with heavy rain, and much thunder and lightning. Made the land off Madras roads, about two o'clock.

July 26th.—Anchored about three miles from Madras, to prevent a heavy squall in the offing from again driving us out to sea. Too late the disembark to-night.

July 27th.—Disembarked from the Warwick with Colonel C. and went to the club, where we got beds and a most excellent dinner from this really magnificent establishment, which, from what I see, appears quite on an equal footing with any of the London clubs. Had Colonel H. Q. M. G. of the Campany's army, to dine with us, and accepted an invitation from him to dinner to-morrow.

July 28th.—Spent the day in delivering my lettees and calling on the different grandees at Madras, and went afterwards to a splendid dinner at Col. H.'s ; after which adjourned to a ball at the public rooms.

July 30th.—Dined at the 63d mess, and afterwards went on board the ship Asia, 1100 tons, bound for Calcutta—a most magnificent ship, and looks still more so after being accustomed to the dingy old Malcolme. I have a good cabin, but without a bed-place ; so that I am obliged to sleep on the floor. Bed places, or, rather, places, in which onc can sleep, are of two kinds ; the one a built structure of wood, the other a cot hung from the cabin ceiling. To all persons going on long voyages, the latter is, to my taste, far preferable, both as taking up less room in one's cabin, and as more easy when the ship is rolling heavily.

July 31*st.*—Sailed from Madras Roads about four in the morning, with a pleasant breeze from the southward.

August 4*th.*—Rainy and disagreeable wheather, with thunder and lightning during the night. Our numerous passengers, who have not made quite so many voyages this year as myself, begin to grumble at the light winds, which so much prolong their voyage.

August 5*th.*—Have at last got the S W. monsoon, and are running before it at the rate of eight knots per hour. High land in sight, off Gausam, on the coast of Bengal.

August 9*th.*—Anchored in the morning off the Sand-heads, but got under weigh again with a strong breeze about twelve o'clock. Entered the river Houghly, and anchored about seven o'clock off Kedgeree, ready for the morning tide.

August 10*th.*—Made sail at half-past six in the morning. Stuck fast off Mud Point. The whole banks of this part of the river were low and swampy, appearing covered, in most places, with luxuriant vegetation and jungle ; though considerable tracts have, of late years, been cultivated, the inhabitants almost disputing, inch by inch, with the wild beasts with which this low country abounds.

August 11*th.*—Succeeded in getting off at last with the tide ; and, after four times heaving up and letting go the anchor, made good our passage to Diamond Harbour, where the vessel arrived about eight o'clock at night.

Met, much to my surprise, about half-way up, Sir Henry Fane, Capt. M., his aide-de-camp, and Dr. W., the staff-surgeon, on board one of the Company's steamers. The strong breeze and contrary tide prevented the steamer catching the Asia before her, arrival at Diamond Harbour, where she and the steamer anchorred. and I went on board, the steamer having turned about with us.

They are going to cruise off Diamond Harbour and the Sand-heads for the benefit of the General's health ; which, I fear, is most necessary, as he looks very thin and ill, and much altered for the worse since I last saw him in England.

I found, on arriving at Calcutta, that Sir Henry intended starting, in a few weeks, on his tour of inspection in the Upper Provinces. An expedition most useful, both to the personal comforts of the commander in-chief and his staff and to the discipline of his army, which, form the heat of the climate, require to be more looked after than even in Europe. This is fortunate, as it will give me time to see some little of Calcutta, and prevent its climate having time to take hold of me.

The life one leads in the City of Palaces is much that of all India—namely, rising two hours before sunrise; a gallop round the course follows, when, consigning both your horse and yourself to the hands of their respective servants, by half-past nine they manage to wind one up for breakfast. By an Indian breakfast by no means must be understood that simple bread, tea, and butter, which compose an English one : on the contrary, it involves among its component parts meat, fish, eggs, omelets; not to mention the eternal curry and rice, which neither breafast nor dinner in this country is complete without. Visiting, scandal (which last abounds in India), and the usual routine of a large English society, kill time till luncheon, or tiffin, as it is called here, which is again a most substantial meal. After this meal, parties generally disperse to their rooms, and amuts themselves as best they may till driving hour (five, or half-past five), which cannot take placc till after the sun is down. At that time a most extraordinary collection of vehicles make their appearance on what is called the course, from the superb "turns out" of the grahdee to the little gig of the Colcutta shopkeeper.

Calcutta, its society, people, and buildings, have been too often described before for me again to do so, and I shall therefore say no more than that dinner-parties are numerous in Calcutta, and the heat of them is only to be compared to changing places with one of the tartlets in the even. Balls and svening parties are far from scarce, at which figure all the new importations of the season ; and, generally speaking, the show of beauty is far from small.

August 18th.—The General came back from his cursie, looking much better, and, I hope, quite convalescent.

August 20th.– Did my first duty as A.D.C., by attending the General in his morning ride.

September 12th.—Employed during the day preparing for our trip up the country, and the noise of boxes nailing and servauts grumbling past bearing. A grand dinner at night, given by the Governor-general in honour of my uncle ; to which all his staff, of course, went, and I among the number. Like all such public parties, more honour than pleasure was received.

September 13th.—Breakfasted with Mrs. P., and started in one of the Governor-General's crrriages ; my uncle and the rest of our party in another, attended by an escort of dragoons ; and proceeded in state through the fort, the streets of which were lined with troops, down to the Gaute. where we all embarked under a salute from the batteries, and arrived safely on board the flat about two o'clock, when she immediately started in tow of a steamer up the river. Arrived at Barackpore, the country residence of the Governor-general, at five o'clock, P.M., and took in the guard. Anchored there for the night. Two brother A.D.C.'s and myself, went ashore, and dined at the mess of the 43d N.I., and remained there till ten o'clock. Re-embarked again, having to get into our boats, carried on men's shoulders down to them, through the mud, about forty yards. Heat abominable during the night. Thermometer 85°.

Septeuber 14*th.*—The flat made sail ; or, rather, the steamer got up her steam, in the morning at dawn, passing along the river at a great rate, with the scenery continually varied. Passed Chinsurah, Houghly, and several villages. Every thing very comfortable on board, and living quite as good as on shore. The flat and steamer, of which the accompanying is a view, are a kind of most convenient passage-boats, under the direction of government, instituted by Lord William Bentinck, and trading once a fortnight between Calcutta and Alahabad, a distance of 800 miles ; being an immense covenience to parties going up the country, and also for parcels. This one was given over exclusively to the use of Sir Henry and his personal staff, the general staff having preceded us to Alahabad. In ordinary trips these boats contain some twenty cabins, all fitted wish Venetian blinds on either side ; so that whatever breeze there may happen to be must blow through, and which in some manner manages to keep off the heat, which would otherwise, at this time of the year, be intolerable.

September 15*th.*—Anchored last night in a strong current, not being able to make further weigh ; and even this morning it was not but great difficulty she was at last made to stem the torrent, which is said to be worse at this time of the year than at any other. Anchored at night off a high bank, for the convenience of the natives cooking, their religious prejudices not permitting them to cook on board ship ; and, unless they can find a bit of ground in which each can make his own fire, nothing but dry peas or flour would these gentlemen touch. Several of us went ashore ; found a quail or two near the village.

September 16th.—Made sail, and passed along the very uninteresting scenery on the banks, the whole of which was almost entirely under water, looking like splendid snipe-ground, but with very little variety ; except here and there fifty or sixty vultures and adjutants devouring a dead body, and some very aguish-looking, half-deserted villages. Anchored at night near a large village but did not go ashore.

September 18th.—Arrived at Behrampore ; a considerable cantonment, containing, at the present time, but one native regiment. The station for the king's troops having been removed from it by Lord W. Bentinck in 1833, the barracks are now much out of repair. We stayed with Mr. M., the collector of the Moorshedabad district, an old friend of the General's.

September 19th.—Sir Henry inspected the regiment, the 4th Native Infantry. A grand dinner in the evening at Mr. M.'s, in honour of Sir H.

September 20th.—Got into Mr. M.'s carriage to breakfast with Col. Macleod, commandant of the Engineers in Bengal, and afterwards to see a palace he is building for the Nawab of Moorshedabad, who formerly was master of great part of Bengal, but who is now entirely without power, and a pensioned servant of the Company, with a revenue of about sixteen lacks of rupees, out of which two are annually taken towards paying the expenses of this palace. It is a most magnificent building, but, I should think, little suited to Eastern manners and habits. It was, however, well worth seeing, and commands a splendid view both up and down the river ; and will in the end, cost 60,000*l.*

The town of Moorshedabad is like all others in this country, very extensive and dirty, containing about 160,000 inhabitants, and was formerly the capital of Bengal under the Mogul emperors. It contains little worth seeing, except, the palace.

Embarked again in the flat after breakfast, and arrived

at about thirty miles above Moorshedabad at night, where two of us went out with our guns, and killed two couple of a kind of black duck, which they say is too strong for Europeans to eat.

September 22nd.—For the first time saw, since I arrived in India, any thing higher than an ant-hill, having come within sight of the hills near Raghmahal—a great relief to the eye after the flat scenery of Bengal. Anchored off the jungle below the town, to which the General and the ladies went to see the ruins of a large palace, formerly the residence of the native chieftain of this district, but now in a state of total decay. I remained behind to sketch. The old palace was built by Sultan Sujah, the brother of Aurungzebe, as his temporary residence. The population of the place is computed at 30,000.

September 25th.—Passed along the river, with the hills in the distance behind us. Several curious rocks in the middle of the river made the scenery of that part of it some of the most beautiful we have yet seen. Anchored, for about an hour, off Baughlerpore, a considerable civil station, and the seat of the collectorate and judge of that division. It is also the head-quarters of the hill-rangers, which the General had intended to inspect, but had not time.

September 27th.—Coal depot ; none forthcoming. Monghir, where we anchored, is situated on the south side of the river, 301 miles from Moorshedabad, with a very extensive fort, which has been celebrated since the earliest period of the Mogul government. It is defended by a tolerably high wall and wide ditch ; the former much out of repair. There are several good European houses within the walls but of which we saw nothing, as the good people here did not send us the wherewithal to see the place : not even so much as a buggy did we get from them. The fort is now merely a depot for invalids, army clothing (the tailors of Monghir being celebrated), and mad sepoys. The sketch on the other page was copied from one taken while we were at Calcutta, and is not at all exaggerated.

September 28th.—Stuck on a sand-bank the whole day, but eventually got off this morning about one.

September 30th.—Anchored in the afternoon off the collectorate of Patna, nearly the largest town in India, situated on the south bank of the Ganges, which is here five miles wide during the rainy season. Patna and its suburbs are stretched along the bank of the river, and, including the latter, take in a distance of nine miles, having one tolerably wide street ; but the remainder of the town built as usual, without order or regularity, and filthily dirty.

Patna was formerly fortified in the Hindoostanee fashion, but the works are now entirely in ruin. There are large quantities of potatoes and other European vegetables grown here, which are eaten both by natives and settlers. It is the seat of the British Court of Appeal, of a city judge and magistrate, of a collector, opium agent, and provincial battalion ; yet the number of European houses is few. Patna contains, of one sect or another, about 312,000 inhabitants ; besides which there is a considerable floating population, consisting of sepoys, camp-followers, and boat men. Patna is 400 miles, by land, from Moorshedabad.

October 1st.—Breakfasted with Mr. T., the head of the Company's opium factory. There was a large party to meet us, and was sat down, about five or six and twenty, to the best breakfest I have eaten in this country. Started from Patna about eleven for Dinapoor, where we are to stay some days.

October 2nd.—Accompanied the General in one of Colonel B.'s carriages to the station church, where the singing would have disgraced an English Methodist chapel. A grand dinner party at General Beecher's, in the evening, to meet Sir Henry.

October 3rd.—Brigade field-day of the 21st king's regiment, and two native regiments, with the usual quantum of firing and noise. Nothing can be finer for their purpose than the whole of the Company's native infantry, and these were good specimens of the force. Sir Henry inspected the two native corps The king's regiment is reserved for tomorrow, as it takes more time than he can spare to day.

Drove in the evening round the environs of Dinapoor, which have nothing very particular in them. The cantonments are handsome buildings, arranged in two large squares, one behind the other ; but they are one story high, and, in point of magnificence, inferior to those of Behrampore. The different barracks scattered through the cantonments are said to have contained, in 1811, 3236 houses. The flag-staff and hospital have a good effect from the river, and make the appearance of the town far superior to Patna.

October 4th.—Left Dinapoor after the General's inspection of the king's 31st regiment.

October 7th.—Anchored off Buxar, Opposite the house of Capt. Mackenzie, who is at the head of the Company's studs in Bengal, one of the most healty-looking places and best cultivated we have yet seen in Bengal. There are about 600 colts on this side, all in the most beautiful condition, kept in long stables, 200 in each. Drove in the evening to see the rickyard and other parts of the stud.

October 8th.—The General inspected the stud on the Coruntidee side of the river ; this large establishment occupying both sides, and its fields and enclosures extending for miles down the river on either bank. There are three establishments of the kind in this Presidency, this being the principal one for horses. The sires are chiefly English, with some few Arabians, and are generally far inferior to what they ought to be for the price the

Comprny give. The mares are all what are called "country bred," that is to say, either mares purely of Indian blood, or bred in the stud itself ; and mares being never admitted into the cavalry, they are almost all turned to breeding purposes.

October 9th.—The Buxar side, which Sir Henry saw this morning, is, if possible, better worth seeing than the Coruntidee ; and one stable in particular, containing 200 colts of three year old, surpassed any thing I had an idea of.

Embarked after seeing these, and started for Gazipoor. Arrived there in the evening, and dined with Mr. Trotter, the government opium agent, who had a large party to meet the General.

Lord Cornwallis is buried here, and has a handsome tomb near the lines, which constituted our evening's drive.

October 11th.—The General saw the rest of the stud this morning, and bought three fine animals for himself. Government for these have the conscience to ask 1000 rupees, or 100 guineas each. This certainly is a large sum, but one must still consider that for this one has the choice of 400 or 500 colts, all in their prime.

October 13th.—Anchored at dark off Benares. The scenery along the banks for the last mile or two has been very beautiful, and nothing can be more picturesque than the City itself, with its temples and minarets, from the river.

CHAPTER III.

Arrival off the Holy City, Benares—Sagacity of the Elephants—A City of Gold—Chunar—Curious Indian Fort—Alahabad—Grand Balls—Amateur Theatricals—Public—Dinners—March Resumed—Futtehpore—Cawnpore—Grand Review—A British Camp in India.

October 14th.—The General inspected three of the regiments stationed at this place ; the prettiest and best-managed brigade I have seen in India. In the afternoon, the whole of us started on seven elephants to see the Holy City, which is certainly the best worth examination of any thing I have yet seen in the East. The streets are so narrow that it is almost impossible to penetrate them on elephants, and as it was, we were obliged continually to dismount and get into tomjons (a kind of open sedan-chair), and let the animals go round.

The houses are, many of them, six stories high, built of stone, each story containing one family, and many covered with execrable paintings of Hindoo gods and worthies of different kinds. In some of the streets the houses on either side come so close as to be united by galleries, and in almost all a good jumper would clear the street with ease. It was wonderful to see how the elephants managed to avoid treading on some of the people, in spite of the immense crowd around them.

The close packing of this place must be extraordinary, as from the top of the mosque (built by Aurungzebe) the city does not appear to extend above a mile any way ; and yet it is said to contain a population of 650,000 inhabitants. This mosque was built on the site of one of the most revered temples of the Hindoos, by the great Mogul, for the purpose of mortifying the Hindoos, and was considered a terrible sacrilege ; but they have now built a temple on the other side of the way, into which they say the god has betaken himself.

Benares is by far the richest city in India, and carries on a very extensive trade with all parts of the Continent, particularly in silks and brocades (commonly called keankabs), which are superb, but very expensive. The European part of the town is small, and stationed at Secoli, several miles from the city.

The faithful Hindoos believe, or ought to believe, that Benares was formerly built of gold, but that in consequence of the sins of its inhabitants it was turned to stone. I suppose they are getting worse and worse, for great part of it is now turned to mud ! The town is considered so holy, that if *even* a Christian were to die here he would most likely go to their heaven.

Benares is about 460 miles by land from Calcutta, and 565 by Moorshedabad.

October 15*th.*—Went through part of the town again this morning, and started afterwards for Chunar, which has an old Indian fort well worth seeing, in which there are some state prisoners confined. It is garrisoned by two companies of N. I. and a detachment of Invalids and Artillery, and commands a considerable prospect towards Benares. The sketch here given is the fort taken from the anchorage.

October 19*th.*—Came to an anchor off Mr. F.'s bungalow, at Alahabad. Passed a guard of honour waiting peaceably in the heat of the sun for the General, whose faces looked rather long than otherwise at finding they had had their labour for nothing ; which, however, could not be helped. as Sir H. intended going on to his brother's house, instead of stopping at the usual landing-place, Alahabad, or rather many of the European houses, are beautifully situated on the banks of the river, which here joins the Jumna ; and the picturesque fort at the confleence forms a fine finish to the landscape.

The house is comfortable, but we do not live there, tents being pitched in the compound. The quiet of a civilian's house and home was sadly disturbed by our arrival ; for, in place of a solitary hurkaru (or messenger) seated at the door, or a single quiet visitors at all hours; orderlies without end ; Adjutant-generals, Quarter-master-generals, and all the *attaches* to an Indian Commander-in-chief ; besides some twenty tents, numerous horses, and all our attendants, placed in the "compound"' or field before the house.

On one of the days we remained, a Mahratta princess staying here sent two rhinoceroses to fight before Sir Henry, who (the rhinoceroses) after punching each other on the head for some time, at last got angry one with the other. The blows got harde and harder, until at last one of the parties thinking he had had enough, turned tail, and ran at the top of his speed through a thick hedge into Mrs. F.'s flower-garden ; where again gaining courage, he faced his opponent, who had followed him : the punching again commenced, and by the time the two brutes could be separated, the place of the garden, or the colour of the flowers, were both most difficult to discover.

October 22nd.—A grand public ball, given by the station to the General ; most pleasant and agreeable, and much larger than I expected, but rather too great a preponderance of the male-sex—a common failing in the Indian ball-rooms. The rooms were excellent, answering both as ball-room and theatre, as occasion requires.

October 24th.—The General inspected the fort, which is well kept and worth seeing, but not defensible against a regular army. It has been partially fortified in the European manner n the land side, and barracks and bomb-proofs made inside. The chief curiosity in it is the celebrated pillar, ascribed by tradition to Bima, one of the heroes of the Mahabarat; but the incriptions on it being illegible, this is all that is known on the subject.

October 26th.—A *reunion* at the public rooms, which was somewhat dull, as there were not many people present ; and those few kept themselves for Mr. F,'s ball on Friday, and would not dance. There ought to be about the best society here of any station in India, as, in addition to the usual district civilians, it is the seat of the Sudder board of revenue.

October 28th.—Mrs. F.'s ball, which went off particularly well, and every body looked happy and comfortable. We kept it up till very late, and I enjoyed it more than any party we have yet been at in India.

October 29th.—Inspection, in the afternoon, of the Artillery; which were small in quantity and indifferent-looking in quantity. No accounts yet of our Buxar horses, which ought to have been here long before this, having started the day after we did.

November 2nd.—The whole party went to the theatre, which is thought by some to be very fine, and would, indeed, be very tolerable, but for the women, whose parts are performed by men ; who, with one exception, are *execrable*, as in all such cases they must be.

November 3rd.—A large dinner party, given by the General in camp, to which I did not go.

November 4th.—Dinner to the General, by the military and civilians of Alahabad. Much less tiresome than I expected. We sat down eighty-two to dinner. Lots of toast-drinking and noise; in the latter, many people thought it necessary to make more than was quite agreeable to the rest of the party assembled.

November 8th.—The General, with his head-quarters and camp, started this morning, leaving myself, Col. B., and some others, to follow in the afternon; a marriage having to take place, which detained some of our party, whose presence was required there. Tents, breakfast things, and everything not absolutely required in the evening, are invariably sent on the night before; and accordingly one always found, on arriving at the new ground, tents pitched, and a home to go into, as if it had never been moved.

November 10th.—I like our present mode of living far better than I expected, as one has no trouble or bother; and, with the exception of getting up in the morning, few disagreeables are encountered. My equipage has increased by several more servants, horses and camels, and will do so to a still greater extent at Cawnpore, when we get our elephants.

The number of servants and people attached to one person surprises those who have never been in the East. My own allowance consisted of an elephant, four horses, eight camels, and twenty domestics: a pretty handsome quantity for one individual!

November 11th. An eleven-mile march, which is just the proper length both for one's horses and one's self, ending near the ancient town of Kurrah; which was formerly a considerable city under the Mogul emperors, but of which little now remains, except the mound on which the fort was built, and numerous ruins of tombs, which surround the town on every side. We rode out to the fort in the evening, passing through a country so intersected with ravines and water-courses as to make it very difficuult riding, particularly with a young horse who does not well understand going down one hill and ascending another.

November 12th.—The longest march we have yet had—fourteen miles and a half; but to a most capital situation, in a magnificent grove of trees, full of parrots, whose unceasing noise nearly stunned me before the day was over.

November 16th.—Futtehpore had the honour of our presence. An ugly country, hot and disagreeable; which did not, however, prevent our taking the usual evening's ride.

Saturday, November 19th.—A short and pleasant march into Cawnpore. The General was met outside the cantonments by all the principal residents of the station, and an escort of the 16th Lancers, one of the thirteen regiments stationed here. They are by far the nicest corps in this Presidency; by all accounts, well mounted, sporting, *young* men: the last qualification rather a rare one in this country of *cidevant* young *militaires.*

Monday, November 21st.—A large and rather pleasant party at General S.'s, the general of division; a good number of ladies of the party, among whom were some of the most celebrated beauties of this part of India. We had two or three quadrilles after the General's deprture, but broke up early for the grand parade to-morrow morning. These said parades at daylight are great drawbacks to the pleasures of a ball, no one dancing with half the spirit when he considers he has to mount his horse for parade in an hour.

November 22nd.—The first grand review of two king's regiments (the 16th Lancers and 16th regiment of Foot), seven regiments of native infantry, and two of cavalry; which, together with a brigade of horse, and another of foot-artillery, made a splendid show. All the world out, of course; most of the ladies on elephants. One of ours, frightened at the firing, turned tail with the ladies, much to their dismay, but returned very quietly afterwards.

The regiments did very well individually, but the Geueral commanding made rather a mess of the matter. All, however, went off very well on the whole ; and, with the exception of the heat, was pleasant enough.

We all went in the evening to the theatre, for which the parties had been foolish enough to choose a sentimental piece, in which the whole point was to be sustained by women, whose characters being represented, the one by a great lout of a horse-artilleryman, and the other by an equally heavy piece of humanity, in the person of a gentleman-officer in one of the infantry regiments, it was, of course, a complete failure, and I cannot say I ever was much more bored. We left it early in the second piece, and were home by eleven o'clock.

November 23rd—The General inspected the 1st and 47th regiments of Native Infantry, from which I made my escape, and slept peaceably till eight o'clock. In the evening all the gentlemen of the party dined at the grand dinner given to the Commander-in-chief by the civil and military of the station of Cawnpore. It was by far the best got-up and arranged public dinner I ever saw : it was laid out in the Assembly Rooms, which were illuminated for the occasion I never saw so large a party ; we sat down upwards of 180 to dinner, but without noise or confusion of any sort.

I may as well give a sketch of our camp here as in any other place, as I shall wish to remember it another time ; as it is always pitched in the same manner, one day describes another :—All the principal tents, that is, those of the Commander-in-chief, his personal and general staff, form a long street of about fifty feet wide, the General's being always in the centre ; the great durbar, or dining-tents, on one side, and the sleeping-tents on the opposite.

This street the Quarter-master-general takes care is always clear of trees, bushes, and other obstructions, and the holes filled up; and that sentries are posred to prevent the intrusion of the *profanum vulgus*, and of those whose ideas on the subject of *meum tuum* are somewhat confused. Behind the lines of great tents are the routys (a smaller kind of second tent for breakfast) and servants' tents; beyond which one's saddle-horses and other cattle stand picqueted in long lines in the open air, in which way they do perfectly well in all weathers in this country. A few people think it better to have their horses under tents, of whom I was one; but this is not by any means common.

At some little distance in rear of the main camp is that of the bazar, separate entirely from the other, where all the rice and trash of all descriptions used by the servants are bought and sold, and of which a nerric, or "price current," is daily given out by the commissary attached to Headquarters.

Quite on the outskirts of all are the elephants and camels, standing enjoying themselves after the long morning's march—about four or five hundred of the first, and seventy or eighty of the last; and near them the long-drilled lines of picqueted dragoon-horses of the escort, with their master's and officers' tents. The infantry are generally placed away from the cavalry, at the opposite side of the camp.

The whole, what with escort and camp-followers of different descriptions, muster nearly 5000 souls, and at times much more, as the camp occasionally varies a good deal in population.

CHAPTER IV.

Cold in India—A Native Chief—Fighting Horses—Anecdote of a Wolf—Indian Partridges—Peacock Shooting—A Character—Curious—Ruins—Visit from two Native Rajahs—Visit Returned—Interior of a Rajah's Dwelling—Antelope Hunting with a Chetah—Joe Manton in India—An Awkward Accident—Mynporee—Shehoobad.

November 25th.—An inspection, in the morning, of two regiments of native infantry, during which one had the pleasure of feeling one's self gradually getting into a kind of icicle without the possibility of moving about. The cold at day-break in this country is often very great ; and, though sounding odd, still I must say, that from the great difference in the temperature between the day and night, I have felt cold more severely in India than in England.

In the eveging the General held a durbar for the reception of the Prime-minister of the formerly great Pashwah of the Maharattas, but now in a kind of honourable captivity at a small town about fourteen miles from this. He came with a very good following,—four elephants and about one hundred horsemen. He was preceded by some dirty-looking vagabonds of hurkarahs, armed with spears ; next, himself mounted on the finest elephant I have ever seen, with his son riding by his side. After them came the remaining elephants, and horsemen armed with long spears, and dressed in the usual quilted armour.

In all native shows of this kind, the jingling of bells, hammering of tom-toms and squeaking of a kind of instrument like a hurdy-gurdy, not to mention the people themselves, make such a noise and confusion as to render it next to impossible to hear one's self speak.

Our visitor stayed about half an hour, talked of himself and his gread exploits, and said he hoped, if any war should break out, that the Commander-in-chief would call upon him for his assistance ; after which came the usual circulation of pawn and attar, and away he went. He is a man of about five-and-forty, with a very good countenance, and has the reputation of being clever and intelligent. His son had one of the finest Mussulman countenances I have seen in this country.

We dined at home for once, and had no one to dinner—a very rare thing with us at a station, the hospitality of India being proverbial.

November 26th—Two more native infantry regiments inspected, the 1st and 45th ; the latter the best-looking corps of those Sir Henry has thus far inspected.

In the evening's ride, a loose horse having frightened the ladies, I gave my own pugnacious gentleman to be held by a soldier, while I attempted to drive the other away. In the meantime the soldier let my horse go, who immediately dashed at the loose one, attacked him, followed him to the lines, and was found with the other brute thrown down and he standing over him.

It is one of the great drawbacks to equestrian exercise in India, this pugnacious propensity, to which all these country horses are more or less addicted ; and it often happens that one is aroused from a pleasant conversation with one's next neighbour by a lion› roar from either his or your horse ; a kick and fight follow, and if one escapes having one's leg broken, it is often at the expense of a bad fall in getting out of the way of the combatants. Shortly before our arrival at Cawnpore, an officer riding in the cantonments was attacked by an artillery horse, that rushed at him, knocked him and his horse over, and killed the former on the spot. Most people, on this account, prefer Arabs to the country horses, as the former seldom or ever are troubled with this quality ; and though small, are, nevertheless, from their blood, equal to almost any weight.

The whole of the last fortnight has been passed in a continual round of morning inspections and reviews, and evening parties, either at home or abroad. To-morrow we again begin our march, much to my delight. Our camp is to be pitched to-morrow at Kullianpore, a short march of nine miles and a-half.

December 9th.—Our first day's march over the worst bit of road we have yet met with, but found the camp pitched on a very good spot, covered with low shrubs, which they say are full of grey partridge, for which I shall beat them this evening.

There are accounts just come into camp of a child of one of the seyces, or grooms, of the escort having been carried off in the most extraordinarily cool manner by a wolf. It was asleep between its mother and father, the former having her arms around it ; and, in spite of this and the immediate pursuit, the annimal managed to get clear off with its prize.

We tried a considerable tract of ground, but without doing any thing but making two or three bad shots at quail, and without finding the promised partridges. The partridges usually found in the plains of India are of two kinds, "the black" and grey ; both, as far as shooting is concerned, giving excellent sport. The former is a very handsome bird, and is much preferred to the other at table ; though, as far as we could make out while in India, both sorts were equally dry and bad when cooked. However, when any of us ventured to express our opinion in this way, it was always said, "Oh, but you have not tasted those shot under the hills, or in Burmah," or at some place where we had never been. Experience has since, however, confirmed this opinion of the birds in all parts of India, both kinds being very far behind the taste of an English one.

December 10*th*.—We started this morning directly after breakfast, with a line of eight elephants, to try what game was to be found on the other side the river. The fording the river and the new character of the country, together with a pleasant cool breeze, would, if we had had but a little more game, have made it a very pleasant day's amusement : but, with the exception of hares (of which we got nine), there was nothing to shoot.

The zemindar, or chief man, of this village, and of eleven more in its neighbourhood, accompanied us the whole day, very well mounted, and armed with a double-barrelled gun, of which he seemed not a little proud. He fired but once, and if that was a specimen of his skill, it was not great, for he did not go within ten yards of his object.

Coming home, Captain M. and I left the rest of the party, and succeeded in getting three peacocks and a brace of partridges to swell our bag ; or rather his, for I never by any chance hit any thing, even of the size of a peacock. There were such numbers of the former, that we shall try for them again on Monday.

In some parts of India, peacock shooting is forbidden by government, the natives esteeming them sacred, and feeding them arouud their villages ; but in this part of the country this was not the case : on the contrary, they seemed rather glad to have them destroyed, the injury they do to their crops being immense. They were in great numbers at this spot, and nothing could be finer than their rise from the ground, and their fall when shot.

December 11th.—Sunday, a halt as usual : most acceptable both to man and beast, the elephants particularly, they having been hard-worked lately.

December 12th.—Captain M. and myself started at daylight for our jungle of Saturday. Found considerably fewer peafowl than we expected, and after a long day's work got but four, and a partridge, having a long ride of fifteen miles (which we did in an hour and ten minutes), in the heat of the sun, as a finisher.

December 13th.—The camp pitched this morning at Merun-k -serai, near the old ruins of the once-famous city of Kanouge, said to have been the capital of India in the time of Porus ; and it was the fame of its wealth that first attracted the attention of the Mahomedan conquerors of India.

We were bothered the whole morning by sellers of what they call old coins, of which there is a manufactory here for those who choose to buy them with gold. The principal man of the party, by name Ouday Ram, shewed me his certificates of character, which, as he could not read them, were somewhat curious. I copied three out of the hundreds which he had, of which the following are specimens :—

"Ouday Ram, the bearer of this, sold me a pot of *bad* tamarind preserve.—D.C.C."

"This old man is a great torment to a sick man.

Again,

"This chap is the plague of mortal man,
His name to many is Ouday Ram,
Well known to all as a cheating rogue,
But, wonderful to say, is much in vogue ;
For travellers honour him with their name,
And I for one add mine with pain,

For he has bothered me with coins sham :
Pray, Burrah Sahib, don't buy of Oudee Ram.
"*September* 23*rd*, 1834."

Most of the characters, however, agreed that he was a very cicerone to shew the ruins ; which he did in the afternoon, and which proved to be well worth seeing—those at least that we had time to look at, which were, however, but a very small part, as the roads were vile, and we were afraid of being in the dark among the ravines and old wells, in which a stray passenger has an excellent chance of breaking his neck.

Friday, *December* 16*th*.—A very short march of six miles into the cantonment of Futtygurh, a small military and civil station, forming the European part of the city of Faroukabad.

In the afternoon Sir Henry held a grand durbar, for the reception of two natives of rank. The first (the young Nawab of the place) came in what is called in state, or, in other words, with as many ragamuffins and as much tinsel as he could collect together *a la mode des Indes* ! Captain C., a brother A. D. C., and myself, went to meet him at the entrance of the camp ; and as we were rather late, he had to wait some little time till we came up, for not one iota of their dignity will these little lords give up ; and if we had not come he would have stayed there all day, as this happened to be the spot where Lord Combermere sent his A.D C. to meet him, and to have come any further would much have diminished his dignity. He was a dull, inanimate-looking boy, of fourteen or fifteen, and looked, during the whole audience, frightened out of his life.

As soon as he had taken his departure, Nawab Montessin al Doulah, commonly called the Hakim Mendes, made his appearance, more in the manner of a private gentleman than the last. He is a very fine old man, with a handsome and pleasing countenance, which well supports his character of being one of the most intelligent and best-read natives in India. He was three years prime-minister of Oude, during which time he is said to have feathered his nest to some prupose, and he is now said to be worth upwards of a million sterling. I wished much to have knocked off his turban, which had an aigrette of diamonds, said to be worth 10,000*l.*; and his shawls were the most beautiful Cashmeres I ever saw. We are to breakfast with him tomorrow morning, which, I am glad of, as I wish to see the interior of a native gentleman's house. His adopted son is to shew the General a chetah kill an antelope tomorrow afternoon.

December 17th—The morning's work began with the inspection of a regiment of native infantry, stationed here; the men of which were decent, and in other respects much like those of the same class.

Immediately after breakfast, we started to eat another of garlic with the Nawab Montessin al Doulah, *alias*, Hakim Mendes, and to return the visit of yesterday. He received the General at the door of his house, surrounded with the innumerable dependents which all natives in this country have always about them, and led the way to the breakfast-room; a long and very fine hall, but much disfigured by having a dirty white sheet thrown across one end, beyond which we were told was a representation of the temple of Mecca.

The breakfast itself would have been good, but for the immense quantity of garlic with which every thing was stuffed. The old nobleman himself talked a good deal, and seemed really affected at the death of Major Maccan, my uncle's late Persian interpreter, whom he seems to have known very well, and to have apprecited. Maccan had been in the same situation with two Commandars-in-chief before my uncle, and had embarked with

Sir Henry in the hope that the climate of India might benefit his shattered constitution—the first time, perhaps, that that part of the world had ever been so honoured. His, poor fellow, was too far gone, and he sunk under it after a residence of some few months in the country.

He (the Hakim) took us afterwards to see his College, of which he is very proud ; but a more ragged or dirty set I have never seen than the pupils in it.

In the afternon we all rode to a plain near the city, where they had an antelope ready, which was immediately turued out before a chetah, or hunting-leopard, the most beautiful animal of his tribe, who was seated blindfolded on a cart. The moment the bandage was removed he dropped quietly off the cart, and, after running the poor devil close for a quarter of a mile, killed him in a ravine.

As soon as this was done we all galloped up, and, after letting him lap some of the blood of the antelope in a ladle, the chetah allowed himself to be blind-folded and led back to his cart, where they treated him to a leg and shoulder of venison for his breakfast. This fun, when after a wild ahtelope, and seen for the first time, is worth beholding; but it soon gets uninteresting, and after we had been out once or twice, we declined being jolted on the hackery, or country cart, on which one is obliged to go and see it.

The son of the Nawab came afterwards to see the Commander-in-chief's guns, one of which, on the tube principle, he seemee very much pleased with, and said he should order out some of the same kind. He is an excellent shot, and three or four years ago he took it into his head he wanted guns, and immediately wrote to Joe Mantou, ordering him to send him ten guns ; for which he enclosed an order for ten thousand rupees, or a thousand pounds.

December 18*th*.—After church this morning (which was in one of the nicest-looking buildings, and best appointed of any that I have seen in India), Sir Henry went in state to return the visit of the boy Rajah of Faroukabad. We mounted our elephants about a quarter of a mile from the entrance of the city, where our host met us with his suite of elephants and hangerson. The town itself and its inhabitants looked clean and well-built; the latter (namely, the inhabitants) particularly well-dressed; every house-top, and even the tops of trees, swarmed with people to see the procession, and among them some of the best-looking women I have yet seen, who, though they take care to hide their faces on all occasions when one meets them in the street, are not always so careful on the house-top; and the brilliant black eyes of these dark beauties are, perhaps, seen to more advantage when viewed in this manner, than if beheld more closely.

The General was received at the entrance by what was supposed to be a guard of honour, in the most ridiculous dresses which it is possible for a human being to conceive, intended to be in imitation of the Company's sepoys. No pen can possibly describe them; all that I can say is, that if they were taken just as they stood and shewn in Bond Street, at a penny a-peep, the showman would make his fortune in a month.

The hall of audience was a noble room, commanding a splendid view from the verandah in front, over the low country, for many a mile. We returned as we went, and I got into a cab, or buggy as it is called here, driven by Capt. C., a brother A.D.C., who proceeded in safety until we got within 300 yards of camp, when he ran foul of a country cart, drawn by six bullocks, and pitched us both in the middle of the road; his horse ran away with the shafts hanging at his heels, and I was the only part of the whole equipage that escaped unhurt—the buggy being smashed all to pieces, the shafts having much injured the horse's legs, and C. having bruise l his arm and put out his wrist. Instead of putting down our upset to his own bad driving, my friend got up and began swearing at the cart driver for running, as he said, against him ; he (C) being going at least fourteen miles an hour, and the cart perhaps one !

December 21*st* —Arrived at Mynporee, a small military cantonment, the native town attached to it being a miserable, ruinous old place, surrounded with a mud wall, now much dilapidated. The General inspected the regiment stationed here in the evening, which was uncommonly well drilled, and in the highest possible order, doing the greatest credit to the commanding officer who had brought it to this efficiedt state.

Commanding officers in this country, who have their regiments in this state, deserve the greatest credit ; as they are often for years at some out-of-the-way place like this, where they have no opportunity of judging of their own corps by others, are seldom inspected, and have nothing but a strict sense of duty to carry them through.

December 24*th*.—The camp was formed near the walls of Shehoobad, under the long range of sand-hills north-east of the city. Sunday, as usual, a halt ; and we rode in the evening to a large garden on the other side, belonging to a rich Hindoo, full of orange-trees and marigolds, but going, like every other thing of the kind in this part of the county, to ruin ; property in this country being so much more divided now than formerly, as to leave but few proprietors who have sufficient to maintain the large gardens, fountains, and pleasure-grounds, which we now see in ruins.

CHAPTER V.

Astonishing Speed of the Antelope—Agra—The famous Fort built by the Emperor Akbar—The celebrated Taj, built by Akbar—New-year's Day in India—Ruins of Akbar's Palace—Exquisite Religious Temple—Futtehpore—Splendid Ruins—Meeting of Pilgrims—Tomb of Mother-of-Pearl—A Day's Sporting—Entry of the Commander-in-chief into Bhurtpore—Its celebrated Defence against Lord Lake and Lord Combermere—Splendid Cortege of the Rajah—State Dinner with the Rajah.

December 26th.—A long march to a very pretty spot of ground, near Farozabad. At one end of the camp were the ruins of a temple, or rather tomb, for such it was, of one of the prime-ministers of the former emperors of Agra ; one of those picturesque and beautiful ruins which make this country so perfect a field for the pencil or brush.

December 27th.—At Etimadpoor. I turned out of the road this morning to chase a broken-legged antelope ; which, however, beat us, although the poor thing's leg was trailing behind it all the way, and we were on thorough-bred Arabs going as fast as they could lay legs to the ground. With dogs one can tire them out, but to attempt coming up with them in any other way is quite hopeless, as the case of this broken-legged one proved.

December 28th.—A long march, of seventeen miles, into Agra ; of which one hears so much in England and elsewhere, and, of course, expects to be much disappointed, as one generally is with Eastern cities. We rode through the streets of the city towards the fort built by the great Emperor Akbar, and supposed to be the finest specimen of Indian architecture, and fortification, in the world. The gates, which are beautifully carved and painted, and the immensely high and embrasured walls, not to mention a ditch, forty feet deep, give it an appearance of strength which, in reality, it does not possess, the walls being too thin to stand long against heavy artillery. The Emperor Akbar, to whom Agra owes all its grandeur, built this fort, surrounding his palace, and though the work was pushed forward with all the vigour possible, it took 1000 labourers twelve years in building

We found the camp pitched on the artillery parade-ground, in a very good place, free from dust, though close upon the city.

December 30th.—The general inspection of the five regiments of infantry, forming the garrison brigade ; which was very much like all others we have seen, neither worse nor better.

The ladies, and all the rest of our party, went in the evening to see the famous Taj ; of which we have heard so much that we are tired of its very name. No conception I had ever formed in my mind, of beauty in architecture, ever came at all near the Taj. It is, perhaps, the only building in the world that no one was ever yet known to be disappointed with. It was built by Shah Jehan, over the remains of his favourite wife Arjemund Banu, *alias*, Muntaza Zemani, or the most exalted of the age. The screen round her tomb is formed of massive cut white marble, inlaid with flowers formed of blood-stones, jasper, cornelian, and a hundred other stones, each more beautiful than the other ; and though the building is upwards of 200 years old, all are in such perfect preservation as to give the flowers the appearance of nature. Some idea may be formed of the beauty of the work, when, in one rose, there are no less than sixty valuable pebbles. In some few places the stones have been extracted, but this rare ; and, since Government have taken it in hand, it is carefully watched. The most valuable of those extracted were taken away by the Jauts, who carried them to Bhurtpore, where the gates of the fort are also supposed to lie buried.

The gardens are beautified with fountains down the centre, and the deep green of the trees shews off, to advantage, the dazzling white of the marble ; of which the whole edifice is built, from the top of the highest minaret to the foundation. The most minute points have been attended to, and even the water-spouts are made of beautifully carved marble. The dome, the highest portion of the building, is some 250 feet high, and the interior of it gives an echo, which has a very beautiful effect.

Some of our party are so taken with this temple that they go morning and evening, and sit in it for hours. This enormous building took twenty years in building, and cost the Emperor 750,000/. It had been his intention to have built a tomb on the opposite side for himself, and connected the two by a marble bridge, which he was only prevented from carrying into execution by death.

For miles, in every direction, the country is covered with ruins of temples and monuments of all kinds, shewing what the magnificence of the Mogul must have been.

We dined in the evening with Sir Charles Metcalfe, the late Governor-general, and now Governor of the north-west provinces. Our party was composed of all the principal residents of Agra, and Sir C. afterwards, with his usual proverbial hospitality, asked the whole party to dine there every day while we remained in the place : which we did accordingly.

January 1st, 1837.—New-year's day in this place does not put one much in mind of old England and all the comforts of home. Nevertheless, one ought to be thankful for having every comfort around one, and preserving one's health in this country of disease.

The next two or three days have been spent in seeing the lions of Agra, and occasional reviews in the cold of the morning, as a variety.

On the 4th, the last day of our stay in Agra, the day's amusements began with a morning parade of two regiments of native infantry (the 36th and 37th), the former a particularly fine one. The cold was intense, the thermometer standing, when we mounted, at 36° between the kurnants, or outer walls of our tents. Great quantities of ice were collected while we remained here, by the usual process of placing a number of small pans, with about an inch deep of water in them, out at night, which in the morning is found to be ice, and is all placed in a mass and beaten together before sunrise. In the afternoon the General inspected the magazines of the fort, which are very extensive, and contain a battering-train of upwards of 100 pieces of cannon, in complete order. The palace was originally formed in three great courts, the first for the imperial guards, the second for the officers of the household, and the third for the private residence of the Emperor and his ladies. The two former are now magazines, while the latter remains in tolerable preservation.

The remains of the palace of Akbar, particularly the Zenana, contain some of the most elaborate and beautiful architecture in the world, the greater part formed entirely of white marble, beautifully inlaid with precious stones ; many of these, however, have been picked out. The audience-chamber, only one side of which remains (the other having been pulled down and sold by auction by Lord W. Bentinck), is, perhaps, its most beautiful part.

It formed a quadrangle, the two ends having beautifully carved fret-work pillars, and the centre being a magnificent open gallery, with the throne in the centre, composed of a single block of black marble, and overlooking the city and country for miles.

We went afterwards to the Motee Musjid (or place of morning worship), one of the numerous beautiful temples with which Akbar filled his favourite city. To my taste this building is even more beautiful than the Taj, being formed entirely of white marble, without colour of any kind, and merely the bordering of the base of the pillars carved in roses in the solid marble. Where the quantity of marble used in the buildings at Agra could have come from is not now known ; but wherever it was, the cost must have been enormous, as nothing like marble exists any where in this part of the country.

We left Agra on the 5th, and on the 6th encamped under the walls of Futtehpore Sicre. This ruined city has the appearance of having been, at some time or other, a place of great magnificence. Akbar built and endowed a tomb here, dedicated to a saint, by the aid of whose prayers he supposed himself to have been blessed with a son ; and some historians have been scandalous enough to suppose that he (the saint) had more to do with it than mere prophecy.

We rode through the ruins of the town in the afternoon, and a more complete scene of desolation I have never seen ; scarcely one stone remaining on another, with the exception of the walls of the city, which seemed to be tolerably entire. The tomb itself was in very fair repair, and the interior presented one of the most lively pictures of Eastern dresses and assemblies I have ever seen, the whole of the great court-yard being filled with people come to the annual fair, which is held on the anniversary of the death of the saint. The burying-place itself was formed entirely of mother-of pearl, with the widows of beautifully carved white marble, looking like the finest lace. From the top of the building we had a very fine view over the country.

We are to make two more marches into Bhurtpore, where we shall be the day after to-morrow.

January 7th.—Great news of the shooting in this neighbourhood. The General and all the party going to try their luck. Antelope, deer, and hogs, in abundance, by all accounts.

The whole party came home at eleven o'clock, with a bag of only two pigs and a deer, the latter killed by the the chetah. The hawks entirely failed, and, altogether, the party seemed less satisfied with their day's sport than any day since we left Alahabad.

We rode in the afternoon through the (misnomered) jungle, a beautiful, open, gladed kind of forest, putting one very much in mind of some of the wilder and least-wooded parts of the New Forest in Hampshire. Deer, antelope, wild hogs, peacocks, and jackals, got up before us in every part, till I began to think that all the game in India was collected on this spot.

January 8th.—The General made his entry into Bhurtpore, the Rajah of which (an independent prince) came to meet him five miles from the town, and to conduct him, in procession, to our new encampment, two miles from the famous fortress in which the Rajah resides.

This place is so celebrated from its having beaten off Lord Lake, and from the determined resistance it make to Lord Combermere this time ten years. The present Rajah, Bulwunt Sing, was attacked, when he was seven years old, together with his mother, uncle, and guardians, by Durpurt Sal, a cousin; the uncle was killed, and the boy confined by the usurper. Lord Amherst tried every means, before resorting to force, to induce the usurper to give way, but without success; and Lord

Combermere laid siege to the place with an army of 30,000 men, and took it after a gallant defence of six weeks. Durpurt Sal and all his family were taken prisoners, and the present Rajah placed on the musnud, or throne.

He has a considerable territory, of about 5000 square miles, over which he possesses absolute power, uncontrolled even by a resident.

The crash of the elephants in meeting of the two suites ; the clouds of welldressed natives, galloping in every direction, with their picturesque-looking dresses and long-tailed prancing horses glancing through the trees of the jungle ; together with the contrast between them and their horses, and the well-mounted and appointed troopers of the escort, formed a scene which far surpassed any thing I have seen, or expect to see, in this country ; I should say that, altogether, he must have had 3000 followers, of different descriptions, in attendance.

The Rajah left us at the entrance to the camp, to return home and prepare for his visit at eleven o'clock. He came with the same crowd of attendants as before, and the whole body of his ministers ; he remained talking for some little time, and offered to send chetahs, hanks, and dogs, for our amusement. He is a jolly-looking, fat gentleman, with a good-natured, though not very clever-looking physiognomy. He attempted the European style, in some degree, and had a carriage and four attached to his *cortege*, and has invited us all to dine with him to-night, at which I expect to be amused.

We started in the General's carriage at six o'clock, and mounted our elephants near the entrance of the town, where the General was met by a deputation from the Rajah, to conduct him into the citadel. The palace was brilliantly illuminated from top to bottom ; and we sat down, about forty, to a very tolerable dinner, served in the English fashion, in a kind of hall, with rows of pillars down the centre, hung with a profusion of chandeliers of every colour in the rainbow. We had five or six sets of Nautch girls, both during and after dinner, all more or less good. The Rajah made himself very agreeable ; and upon the party breaking up, we were all loud in praise of the prince.

The two remaining days of our stay at Bhurtpore were spent by the General, and most of the party, in capital snipe and wild-fowl shooting on the lake. Two of our party killed 112 head in two days.

CHAPTER VI.

Departure from Bhurtpore—Hunting with Chetah and trained Deer—Deig—Its faded Grandeur—Splendid Royal Gardens—Military Stations—The Birthplace of the God Krishna—A Disappointment—Racing by celebrated Arabians—English superior to Arab Racers—Meerutt—Splendid Review—Superiority of the Company's Horse-Artillery—The Public-dinner Nuisance—State Party—The celebrated Begum Sombre—A Suicide by Mistake—Buried Alive—Letter from Runjeet Sing.

January 12*th*.—A short march out of Bhurtpore, and the Rajah has sent three chetahs and several hawks and hunting deer, to accompany us through his territory.

The chetah hunting I have already described, and here I shall only say, that, in this instance, we killed several deer in the forest, they allowing us to get near enough, when seated on one of the country carts, to the sight of which they are accustomed. It is beautiful to see the leopard sneaking down from the cart, taking advantage of every little bush and shrub to hide himself, and, just at the moment the deer begin to be alarmed, making four or five desperate jumps, which bring him up with one, whose throat he is upon in a moment, and its life-blood sucked from its veins. After this exploit the chetah invariably allows himself to be quietly caught.

The hunting-deer are very curious ; and I do not remember to have seen them in any other part of India.. A large male antelope is trained to walk quietly among a herd of wild ones, one of the males of which immediately comes out to fight. The tame one having ropes twisted in a particular manner among his horns, soon manages to entangle his antagonist ; and the moment he finds he has done so, he throws himself on the ground and anchors the other until people come up and secure him.

The buck we tried it with dashed immediately at his opponent ; but the other smelled that something was wrong about the tame gentleman, and started off as fast as his legs could carry him. The natives said this was rare, and that they generally managed to secure the wild one.

January 13*th.*—Marched into Deeg, which has the appearance of having been once a very large and flourishing place. The extent within the walls is enormous. The only parts now worth seeing are the gardens attached to the palace, which are still kept by the Rajah as a residence during the rains The water-works are well worth seeing, and far surpass those those of the Taj, both in extent and beauty. The town and fort were stormed and taken by Lord Lake, in 1804, many of the enemy having thrown themselves into it after the defeat of Holkar.

The country in the neighbourhood seemed most unhealthy and malaria-looking. There is a considerable lake close to the town, and a smaller one near yesterday's encampment-ground.

January 16*th.*—A long march of fourteen miles into Muttra, a small military station, with the 10th Cavalry and a brigade of horse-artillery quartered in it ; encamping on excellent ground on the old infantry parade. In the afternoon the General inspected the cavalry stables, and the remainder of our party rode round the environs, which were nothing extraordinary.

January 17*th.*—A review of the 10th Cavalry and the troop of horse-artillery ; the former the finest cavalry regiment we have yet seen —very steady, and in uncommonly good order.

We started in the carriage to go seven miles, over a most execrable road, to see the Hindoo temples of Bindrabund, which were said to be worth seeing. Bindrabund being the scene of the birth and early adventures of their favourite god Khrishna, and, of course, being one of the most holy cities in India, was equally certain of being one of the most dirty, and filled with vagabonds in the shape of fakirs, monkeys, Brahminy bulls, and peacocks. These bulls have the largest stock of easy impudence of any animals I ever met with, coolly pushing people out of their way in their passage down the streets ; and neither the dignity of the great man, nor the insignificance of the small, can persuade them to budge one inch from what they seem to consider as their right —the best place in the street. After having nearly every bone in one's body broken by the jolting of our palanquin carriage over these execrable roads, and being afterwards nearly suffocated by the narrow, low streets of the town, we gained nothing but the sight of an indifferent ruin and the view of a dirty-looking idol.

Head-quarters left Muttra on the 18th, and made a short march to Rao.

January 20*th.*—Encamped on a wretched piece of ground behind an indigo factory, near Kaku, with a high wind blowing the sand into one's tent the whole day. This is one of the greatest annoyances in Indian marching ; for in the course of an hour or two after one's tent is pitched, it, and every thing belonging to you, becomes one mass of dust.

Jannary 21*st.*—Entered the cantonment of Allyghur, the head-quarters of a regiment of infantry, and a small military station. I had a hard gallop of fifteen miles to be up in time (eight o'clock) to see the rces which are going on. I was in time to see the last race, between the Borderer, the most celebrated Arab of his day, and another. The race was pretty good, and heavy bets depended on it.

Racing is carried on in India to a great extent, chiefly by Arabians, though of late English horses have come in, and carry off most of the larger stakes; for though, in a long race, the bottom of the Arab will give him an advantage, still the stride of an English horse is not to be got over.

This place was formerly the head-quarters of the French general Perron, under the Mahratta Government, and one of his largest magazines. The fort, or rather the walls of it, still remains, but the interior has not a vestige of any building with the exception of some modern deserted magazines. The walls are faced with stone, and the ditch, in some places, is so wide that a flock of wild fowl swimming in the middle would be out of shot from either side. It was stormed by Lord Lake in 1803, and only taken after considerable loss had been sustained on our side. The enemy had neglected to break down the bridge, which the Commander-in-chief took advantage of, and, under a heavy fire, succeeded in gaining possession, killing the governor and 200 of his men.

January 24th.—Heavy thunder-storms during the night have drenched every thing belonging to us, from our horses downwards. Altogether, this is the most disagreeable day I have yet passed in camp. This camp is a mass of mud, and one's tent steams like a wash tub.

A wet day under canvass is a general nuisance; it makes every one look sulky and disgusted; horses hang their heads and look wretched; sernants roll themselves in their blankets and will do nothing; the cold is abominable, and one's feet get wet in going from one tent to another. Happily, in India rainy days (exceptnig in the season) are both few and far between; and one thinks one's self most unlucky if one has half-a-dozen wet days in the course of one's march.

February 1st.—A general inspection of the king's 11th Light Dragoons, now on their route towards Cawnpore, so as to be ready to embark for England, their time of service being expired, and the 3rd Dragoons every day expected to relieve them from Indian service. The regiment was more beautifully mounted than any corps I ever met with.

The Commander-in-chief was met about three miles out of Meerutt by the two generals and all the staff of the place, to escort him to his tents. General Ramsay (a brother of Lord Dalhousie), the commanding officer of the division, being of the party.

We are to dine peaceably at home tonight and to-morrow; after which our gaieties commence.

This station is the most popular and most pleasant, as well as most comfortable-looking, in India, and the force stationed here is the largest and best-appointed collected at any one post in Bengal, with the exception of Cawnpore.

Friday, February 3rd.—The first general review of all the troops in Meerutt. Of course all the beauty and fashion of the place on the ground. The whole mustered about 3500 men, and with the horse-artillery and dragoons made a really splendid show. The plain is a much better one than that of Cawnpore, well covered with grass, and without dust; and though there were some few *faux pas,* it, altogether, went off very well. The horse-artillery (the finest arm of the Company's forces) is here seen in perfection, and, if possible, is superior to our own in Europe.

Saturday, February 4th.—The most delightful of all amusements, turning out at daylight to a review of the horse-artillery and 2nd Cavalry, which was so well worth seeing as *almost* to compensate for even such a sacrifice. The horse-artary [illegible]; particularly well mounted, having the second choice of hor are that is, when the young horses, which are annually sent from the studs for remounting the cavalry and artillery, are collected together, a committee is ordered to inspect them, and if found sound, the first choice is given to the European dragoons, being the heaviest, the second to the horse-artillery, and the remainder to the Company's cavalry.

Tuesday, February 7th.—Allowed to sleep on in peace till eight o'clock, without being disturbed by review or inspection. A large state party in the evening, of which, as aide-de-camp in waiting, I was doomed to be one.

February 8th.—Our last day in Meeruit, fully taken up with paying bills and making arrangements, and the evening in a large dinner-party at home, and a ball afterwards given by the station to General S.

Thursday, February 9th.—Left Meerutt on our way towards Kurnaul, and marched towards Sadanha, the former place of residence of the Begum Sombre. This celebrated woman, who died about two years ago, was a half-caste, and originally married to Colonel Dyce, a German, who obtained during the civil wars of India, after the downfal of the Great Mogul, and before our taking possession of the country, one of the many small principalities into which the whole empire was subdivided. Aware of her husband's love for her, she pretended, on a threatened invasion of his territories by the Mahrattas, to destroy herself, and caused a pistol to be fired near her palanquin. The plot succeeded. Her spouse said he would not survive her, and shot himself through the head, when she immediately seized the government, soon became one of our closest allies, and was confirmed in her usurpation, which she retained till her death, when, according to treaty, it lapsed to our government.

She seems to have been a strange mixture of good and evil. On the side of the former, she is said to have been kind to her people, and a good mother to her adopted children. On the other, it is argued that she was arbitrary, avaricious, and at times cruel. The worst story told of her is her having been jealous of a Nautch girl, to whom her husband had paid rather too much attention, having her buried alive, and seating herself above the place, smoking her hookah The Europeans about her, however, deny the story, and say that, except to culprits, she was never cruel.

She built and endowed a Roman Catholic chapel, which is very beautiful, inlaid like the Taj, the whole of the interior being of white marble. She is said to have died worth nearly 500,000/, which is all left to Mr. Dyce Somber, her son-in-law, who is just gone to England with it.

The following letter from Runjeet Singh, the king of Lahore, as he is called, was received while we were coming up the country, and it was upon this invitation that our subsequent visit to Lahore. took place :—

Translation of a letter from the Mahah Rajah, Runjeet Singh, of Lahore, to his Excellent General, Sir Henry Fane, G.C.B., Commander-in-chief in India. February, 1837.

By the Grace of Siree Akalpoorkah Jee.

Friendly and kind Sir, favourable to friends who are the mark of unanimity, and sincerity, Hail !

After relating the extent of my desire, which, like the noble qualities of your Excellency, surpasses description and limit, be it made known to your illustrious mind, the picture of friendship !

Since, by the grace of Siree Akalpookah Jee, the two exalted states are celebrated for entire unity, and connexion, and friendship, and intimacy, agreeably to the established engagements of amity, and sincerity, and unanimity, and concord, between the two higq courts, according to treaties settled for ever, and fixed and established of old, and are thus as well known to the world, and to the inhabitants of the world, as the eternal light of the sun ; and since, from hearing your Excellency's exquisite virtues and noble qualities, which form a conjunction of friendship, my mind, which is the emblem of sincerity, has been greatly gladdened, and delighted, and rejoiced, and my heart, the resting-place of friendship, according to the strong, and ancient, and pure intimacy between the two states, became desirous of an interview, the sign of delight, with your Excellency of eminent merits, agreeably to old and firm engagements ; how that in these days, marked by prosperity, the marriage of my happy son, the rest of my soul, the friend of fortune, the brightness of the forehead of felicity, the pupil of the eye of dominion, the light of the sight of immence prosperity, the bud of the garden of sovereignty and glory, the Prince No Nehil Singh, with thousands of happy and prosperous omens, will complete the picture of my desire ; and you, sir, entirely excellent, by a fortunate coincidence, have honoured and bestowed splendour on Hindostan, in your visit to the English cantonments; therefore, it is written with the pen of the string of friendship, that if your Excellency also, through your amiable and friendly qualities, will add to this friendly meeting new delight and unbounded happiness by your presence at this fortunate marriage, in these days connected with prosperity, agreeably to established engagements, I should conceive the greatest pleasure and double delight. I beg that you will always believe that my heart, the sign of friendship, is anxious for news of the health and prosperity of your Excellency, and that you will, by writing and sending them, bestow pleasure on my mind, which is the resting-place of unanimity !

Given in the days of Spring, the emblem of happiness, and in the month of Phirgoon, 1893.

CHAPTER VII.

Crossed the Jumna to Kurnaul—State Dinner and Ball—Delays and Difficulties – Quarrels of the petty Rajahs—Ambala · Sirhind—Visit from a Rajah –Visit Returned—Loudiana – A Colony of Cashmerians—The Cashmerian Women no Beauties – Messenger from Runjeet Sing—Passage of the Sutlej—Striking Scene– Son of Runjeet Sing – Official Visit—Solecism in Indian Manners—Stete of Cultivation of the Sutlej – Official Visit Returned—Nattve Artists—Shere Sing's Dressing-room—Ancient Capital of the Seikhs—Deputation from Runjeet Sing—Unequalled Splendour of Dress—Magnificent Scene—Kumuk Sing.

February 15th—Crossed the Jumna over an indifferent ferry, and encamped on the opposite bank, and the following day entered Kurnaul. The General was met, as usual, on entering a station, by General Duncan, commanding the division, and all the staff of the place. This station is usually a popular one, and considered one of the most healthy in India. We dined this evening with General Duncan, who had a numerous party to meet us, and adjourned afterwards to the public rooms, where we found a well-filled ball-room in honour of Miss F. With the usual hospitality of the East, invitations to balls and parties had been sent to us some days before; but being in haste to be at

Lahore, Sir Henry pushed on, and thus at this time prevented our seeing much of the Kurnaul society.

February 17th.—A review of the Kurnaul brigade; after which we breakfasted with General D. and his family, who have a noble house here built for Sir D. Ochterlony. The rain, which began while we were at breakfast, continued during the eleven miles' march to our next halting ground. Our camp, which was pithed near the village of Seetakheree, was one mass of mud.

February 18th—Happily the rain has ceased, and hopes are entertained that we may not be obliged to halt, and thus be too late for the wedding at Lahore. Camels and bullocks knocked up in every direction on the road, the rain having turned the heavy sand into mud and made it next to impassable. One's baggage on a rainy day often stands a great chance of being left on the road ; for if carried on camels, the chances are much in favour of their slipping down on the mud, and even of splitting themselves up ; and if in a "hackery" (or native cart), the chances are still greater of its sticking fast, when your servants are certain to sit down and smoke "the pipe of patience," leaving Providence to get the cart and its contents out.

February 20th.—Entered Amballah, a considerable and flourishing town, the residence of the Governor-general's political agent with the Seikh states. They are most of them good riders, and are considered the best irregular cavalry, with the exception of the Mahrattas in India. They are, generally speaking, an active, warlike race, as different from the indolent and apathetic Hindoo as an inhabitant of the northern parts of Russia is from the Turk. The political agent (Mr. Clerk) has a most difficult card to play to keep peace between all these petty rajahs, who constantly get into hot water, one with another, if not closely watched.

February 22nd—Head-quarters entered Sirhind, formerly one of the largest cities in India, but now having scarcely one stone remaining on another. In the evening the General received the

Patialah Rajah, the most considerable chief on this side of the Sutlej, with a revenue of nearly thirty lacs of rupees (3,00,000*l*.). He came with a very good following of twenty or thirty elephants, and six or seven hundred horsemen. I was too late for the durbar, finding coursing hares better fun.

February 23rd.—The General returned the visit of the Patialah Rajah, for which this day's halt, the only one between Kurnaul and Umritsir, has given him so good an opportunity. We passed through a double line of horsemen, whose files extended half a mile, into a large walled garden, into which were pitched the tents of this worthy. The Patialah Rajah himself was the largest man I almost ever saw, standing, I should think, six feet seven or eight, with bone and sinew in proportion. He was surrounded by his children and courtiers, and gave us one of the best Nautches I have ever seen. After the durbar, a quantity of things was produced : among them a beautiful suit of armour, as a specimen of his country manufacture, and as a present to the chief. These, of course, he could not accept, and the only article he took was a small but beautiful bow, worth some five or six rupees.

February 25th.—Encamped near the walls of a large serai, with its doorways beautifully enamelled ; one of that fine line of similar buildings built by the Moguls for the use of travellers between Delhi and Lahore. We rode in the evening through it, in spite of the staring of the Seikhs at the sight of the unveiled ladies of the party. It was a picturesque-looking build, partly in ruin, and would have made a perfect picture with the warlike-looking natives, and their long-tailed showy horses and varieties of dress, backed up with the dark masses of the place, thrown well into shade by the declining sun. The whole neighbouring country was the most uninteresting we have yet seen—a dead flat, but without even the usual relief to the eyes of occasional clumps of trees.

February 26th.—A long march through a desolate, jungly-looking country, the latter part over the ancient bed of the Sutlej, into Loudiana, the most northern station of our Indian empire. Loudiana is situated in what appears to have been an island in former times, having nullahs, or water-courses on three, and the old bed of the river on the fourth side. It is a most *triste* and desolate-looking place. A very large proportion of its population are Cashmerians, driven by Runjeet's exactions to quit his territories, and have set up here a considerable manufacture of shawls on their own account.

We hear at this place that the marriarge *fete* at Umritsir is to last thirteen days, and that the Rajah has made up his mind to spend thirty lacs of rupees (3,00,000/-) on the occasion.

If the Cashmere ladies we saw this morning are specimens of the beauty of the celebrated women of this country, it is not great ; for a dirtier or uglier set of females I never saw, and their habitations seemed, if possible, more filthy than themselves.

The two regiments stationed here of native troops were inspected in the evening.

February 27th.—A long march of fifteen miles through a deep sandy road, to Poondi, on our way towards Hurreekee, where the Commander-in-chief is to be met by a deputation headed by the Runjeet Sing's son, Shere Sing, to conduct him to Lahore.

Our march has lain this morning parallel with the Sutlej, through a low, aguey-looking country, probably impassable in the rains. On the march we met a Vakeil from the Rajah of Indore, sent to congratulate the Commander-in-chief on his arrival in his country, and to continue with him during his stay in it. Two trumpeters, which he had with him, played "God save the King" as the General rode up. His troops were well-dressed—in crimson light-dragoon jackets and trousers, with turbans ; and armed with match-locks, swords, &c. &c. They seemed very tolerably mounted. The words of command were given in Freneh, and, for the first time since I left France, I heard the "*en avant*" of the French dragoons.

February 28*th.*—Our road this morning (if such it can be called) was a miserable footpath along the southern bank of the Sutlej, dreadfully heavy for hackeries (country carts) and horse-artillery. For the first time we came in sight of the river.

March 2*nd.*—Encamped within four miles of the Sutlej, preparatory to the difficult passage to-morrow and the meeting with the deputation of Runjeet Sing, after which we are to encamp on the opposite bank, in the Mahah Rajah's country.

Four or five different parties went out shooting to-day, in different directions, and with various success, some killing as many as sixteen brace of black partridge and eight hares, on the road between yesterday's and today's encampment.

Orders are given that the troops precede the General in the morning, and form on the opposite bank, to receive him when he lands.

March 3*rd.*—The passage of the Sutlej. This morning was one of the prettiest scenes I have ever witnessed in this or any other country. The stream at this part of the river must, in the rains, be from two to three miles wide, but at this season is contracted to between 200 and 300 yards; in some parts it is thirteen or fourteen feet deep. The liveliness of the scene, with the embarkation of the cavalry, horse-artillery, and baggage, the long lines of the escort formed on the right bank, and in the distance the crimson tents and picturesque figures of Runjeet's deputation, backed up by the high bank and ravines to their rears, presented a picture which few have an opportunity in their lives of witnessing far exceeded my expectations.

A large pinnace was in waiting to receive the Commander-in-chief and his staff, which took us in the moment we left our horses. The boats used for transporting the cavalry and baggage were long flatbottomed ones, with high prows, probably of the same kind in which Alexander the Great made the passage of this river ; when the said high prows were useful in defending the passengers in the boats from being annoyed by arrows, aimed at them from the banks. All the troops passed without difficulty or accident, with the exception of two artillery horses drowned ; one of which was kicked over the side of the boat by his neighbour, and the other jumped over, and was drowned by entangling himself in his harness.

As soon as the chief landed he was met by Shere Sing (Runjeet's son), under tow of Captain Wade, the Loudiana political agent. The Seikh chief was as handsome a black-bearded gentleman as one often sees, richly dressed in silk and brocade, and followed by several hundred attendants, of different degrees, most of them dirty ragamuffins, but some few of them well mounted and armed. His infantry (a part of Runjeet's regulars) seemed but indifferent ; and if his regular battalions are no better than the specimens we saw this morning, one regiment of Sepoys might disperse any number of them without much difficulty. Though reported to be the Maha Rajah's son, Shere Sing's father has never thoroughly acknowledged him, though his mother always insisted on his being so. A brother of Shere, by the same mother has been even worse treated than himself, not being permitted to appear at court, and no office given him, either of profit or honour. His influence might have been great, were it not for his expensive and debauched habits, which keep him continually poor, and prevent his having the chance of succeeding to his father's throne which he might otherwise have.

The Seikh chief rode with the General to his camp, about two miles from the river, where the troops marched past him down the main street. The turban peculiar to this tribe is a great disfigurement to this otherwise handsome race ; it covers the whole of the forehead, and gives the face a low, undignified appearance, which it really does not properly possess. The dress usually worn by the chiefs is handsome and becoming ; consisting of the said turban, with a small plume s'uck in the front, (much in the same way as the Highland chiefs in Scotland place a heron's feather in their bonnets) ; a short jacket, generally made of silk, handsomely embroidered, and trousers made wide at the keen, and fitting close round the ankle, of gold or silver kingcob, with a dagger stuck in the belt, often covered with precious stones. We afterwards found that the trouser fitting tight at the knee was the more common costume, the loose one being an innovatian lately introduced by the heir-apparent, and now beginning to be adopted by the dandies of the court of Lahore.

Shere Sing, while with us this morning, fixed to pay his official respects to the Commandes-in-chief this afternoon, and about four o'clock made his appearance, with a very good suwarree, or following. He gained the very favourable opinion of all during the visit by his quiet and gentlemanly manners, and his perfect good nature. He had the most beautiful tiara of diamonds, emeralds, and rubies, I have almost ever seen ; some of the emeralds, in particular, being enormous, and probably of great value. His second in the deputation, Said Khan (the man who was sent to meet Burnes on the Indus), is, if any thing, a handsomer man than himself ; though he has not the same gentlemanly manners, or quiet good nature. He committed that great breach of Eastern decorum, entering the presence with his shoes on, which is sufficient to damn him, in the opinion of the old Indians, to the end of the chapter.

This entering the presence, even of an equal, in this country, is universally considered as the greatest of insults,—the shoes in the East being considered in the same light as one's hat in our own country. One's servant never would dare to do such a thing - one's equal would have a similar feeling on the subject; and in a case like the present, where it was an inferior sent to greet a superior on the part of his master, it was an atrocity rarely met with. However, it was too important for all parties to keep on good terms for any notice to be taken of the matter, and in this case it was passed over in silence.

He stayed about half-an hour, and then took his departure.

March 4th—To our great disgust, both chiefs and all their followers accompanied the General during the whole morning; and with the neighing and prancing of their horses, and the confusion they caused, set our horses off, and made them unbearable, not to mention the chance one had of being kicked in the scramble.

There is a marked difference in the cultivation on this and our own side of the Sutlej, the advantage being ten to one in favour of our own. Villages are few and far between; and what there are appear to have but few inhabitants, and these few seem without industry or any visible employment. This state of things must not be entirely laid to Runjeet's door, but rather to the prejudices of the Seikhs, who think that all labour but that of a soldier is a disgrace, and who would sooner starve than cultivate their fields.

The General returned Shere Sing's visit of yesterday, in the afternoon. We found his tents pitched in the centre of a large field of standing corn, and all his cavalry and infantry formed up in it, without the least compunction. No native can understand that he has no right to drive or ride over the crops of his neighbour, and in the purely notive states, artillery, horses, and in fact the whole line of march, walk through standing corn, and pitch their tents in it, without troubling their heads touching the owner's feelings. In our own territories the Company have taken the most effectual way of preventing the same thing—making every man pay for the damage he commits, and every officer responsible for his men. He (S. S.) met the Commander-in-chief at the entrance to his own tent, and conducted him to the durbar, formed in a small but beautiful one, with an awning, pitched at one end of the large of Kurnauts, probably enclosing half an acre of ground.

During the whole time we were there a native *artiste* was very quietly standing in front of the two chiefs, taking the General's likeness, making him more like Sir C. Metcalfe than any thing else.

We went afterwards into Shere Singh's dressing-place of which he seemed very proud. It was filled with looking-glasses, French scent-bottles, and little knick-knacks of all kinds, and evidently shewed the master to be a dandy of the first water. His fondness for European luxuries is not confined to the toilette; for, if report speak truth, wine by him is by no means despised, and a European carriage always follows in his train.

March 5th.—This being the appointed day for our entry into Umritsir, the ancient capital of the Seikhs, where Runjeet is now residing, we were met half way on our short march (five miles) by the Maha Rajah's eldest son, Kurruck Sing, and his prime minister, to congratulate the Commander-in-chief on his arrival, and conduct him to his camp. He brought an offering of 5,000 rupees; and both he and all his suite literally blazed in jewels, and cloth of good and silver.

The most striking figure in this deputation was Diahn Sing, the prime minister, and most powerful person in the Punjab. He was superbly mounted on a large Persian horse, who curveted and pranced about, as if proud of his rider. His bridle and saddle were covered with gold embroidery, and underneath the latter was a saddle-cloth of silver tissue, with a broad fringe of the same, which covered his horse to the tail ; the horse's legs and tail were dyed with red, the former up to the knees, and the latter half way up, as an emblem of the number of enemies he had killed in battle, and that the blood from them had covered the animal thus far.

The chief himself was dressed with the utmost Seikh magnificence, covered with jewels, which hung, row upon row, around his neck, in his turban, on the hilt of his sword and dagger, and over all his dress ; while a French cuirass, some hundreds of which General Allard had brought from France, shone upon his breast.

Kurruck Sing and many others were superbly dressed, but none could compete for a moment with this grandee, who, in addition to his superb equipment, adds a face and person seldom surpassed. He is an independent chief in his own country (the mountains bordering on Cashmere), as well as prime minister in the Punjab, and can, it is said, brieg at need 10,000 men into the field.

The meeting between the deputation and our party was, of itself, worth coming to see. The Seikh party consisted of from 2,000 to 3,000 horsemen, all splendidly turned out, in every colour of the rainbow, and extending half a mile on either side of the road. The crush at the junction was, as may be supposed, pretty considerable, and it was as much as one could do to keep one's horse from fighting his neighbour, while staring about to see the fun.

Kurruck Sing, the eldest son of Runjeet and father of the bridegroom to whose marriage we are now going, is not nearly so good-looking as his brother, nor has he the same good-natured expression ; but among his countrymen he is considered learned, because he is the only one of the family who can read and write.

We left Umritsir on our right, passing Runjeet's principal fort of Gobind-Ghur, where all his treasure is deposited. His artillery thundered from the walls, in every direction, as we passed. The cannon seemed to be entirely on the bastions, and fired without much order or regularity.

After arriving in camp and dismissing the infantry, the General took down the cavalry and horse-artillery and saluted the Maha Rajah with a royal salute of twenty-one guns, at which we heard the old man was much pleased. His tents we could see at a distance, distinguished from the rest by a golden ball on the top, the scarlet "purdahs" which surrounded them, and the line of sentries around. We then returned home to breakfast, and to dress and prepare for the forthcoming ceremony.

CHAPTER VIII.

Meeting between Runjeet Sing and the British Commander-in-chief—Extraordinary Scene of Splendour—The Reigning Favourite—Interchange of Presents—Marriage Ceremony and Presents—An Awkward Predicament—A Royal Scramble—Enormous Crowd—Wonderful Sagacity of the Elephant—The Bridegroom—The Ceremony—The Fireworks—The Dancing-girls—Passing the Glass—Distribution of Largess—The Bride's Dowry—"Sport" in the Punjab—Indian Illuminations—Visit to the Rajah's Private Gardens—Runjeet Sing's Visit to the Commander-in-chief—His Admiration of the English Cavalry—His Sagacious Questions—Extraordinary Religious Sect.

At eleven we all again started for the General to pay his visit of ceremony to Runjeet, at his garden-house, about a mile from our encampment. His party met ours about half way, and we all formed and proceeded towards his house in state. The two parties made, altogether, near seventy elephants ; himself and most of his court dressed in yellow, and surrounded with clouds of both horse and foot ; but neither dresses nor soldiers could be looked at while the lord of them all was present, all eyes being too much occupied with him to trouble themselves with any thing else

The lion of the Punjab is a very small, infirm-looking, old

man of fifty-five (looking ten years older), but still more hale and stout than I expected to have seen him from what we had previously heard. He was dressed very plainly in green Cshmere turban, coat, and gloves, with single rows of large pearls down the breast, round his neck, and on his arms and legs, and a single string of very large diamonds round his arms. The Seikh turban, which so much disfigures the whole of this handsome race, does so particularly with him, and gives his countenance a low expression of cunning, which it would not probably otherwise have. His single eye is bleared and bloodshot, but still shews that wonderful acuteness and determination by which he has been able to subdue the unruly spirit of his people, and still to keep them in the most abject subjection. The two parties having met, Sir Henry left his elephant and took his seat beside the Maha Rajah, for which purpose the animals are brought side by side. The operation is a somewhat dangerous one : for, should the animals move away at all from one another, the chances are in favour of your slipping between, and getting a fall of some ten or eleven feet. In this instance, however, no such misfortune happened, and the two great men journeyed on amicably to Runjeet's durbar.

A paralytic stroke, which Runjeet Sing received some fourteen months ago, has much impaired his powers of speech, and all he says is obliged to be repeated by those around him, and so on to the interpreter. This seemed to annoy him much, and to to keep him in continual fear, lest the General should find it out.

We found his dusbar, or place of assembly, erected under a canopy in front of the small house in which he was residing ; the canopy was formed of beautiful Cashmere shawls, inlaid with silver, and with silver poles to support it. The floor was also covered with shawls. The dresses and jewels of the Rajah's court were the most superb that can be conceived ; the whole scene can only be compared to a gala night at the Opera. The minister's son in particular, the reigning favourite of the day, was literally one mass of jewels ; his neck, arms, and legs, were covered with necklaces, armlets, and bangles, formed of pearls, diamonds, and rubies, one above another, so thick that it was difficult to discover anything between them.

Singularly enough (particularly in the East), the father *stood* always in the Rajah's presence, whereas the son *sat* on his left hand. There was scarcely any one present that was not covered with jewels to several thousand pounds' value. This may seem curious to the uninitiated, but it must be remembered that the whole wealth of the country is in the hands of a few, and that of those few the most part were present on this occasion The old prince talked away at a great rate, discussed many subjects, and asked questions of all kinds, many of them shewing his shrewd and calculating character. The size of the Company's army—the number of battles Sir Henry had been in—the number of English officers attached to each regiment—our mode of casting artillery—were some of his many questions.

After the durbar the presents were brought out, and the Rajah presented an offering of 5,000 rupees in money. He afterwards brought his stud for the Commander-in-chief to look at, and presented him with five horses of different kinds. There was nothing remarkable in any of the Rajah's horses, though for one of them he had fought five campaigns, and expended the lives of 20,000 men ; or, rather, the horse was made the excuse for a war, not the most justifiable, which ended in Runjeet's conquering, though not till very large losses had been suffered on both sides.

Our day's work could not be finished without another turn-out, so we again started with the Maha Rajah to see the ceremony of the presentation of the marriage presents to the bridegroom, by the different chiefs of the court, and by the Rajah himself. The ceremoney took place in a house of one of his sirdars, and was more curious than amusing.

Among the party collected were upwards of eighty Nautch girls, some three or four of whom were really beautiful women, but the great body quite the reverse.

All the Rajah's nobles and chiefs presented their offerings to the bridegroom, one after another ; and their presents altogether were valued at nearly 17,000/- which will go some little way towards paying the marriage expenses.

We were there nearly two hours, and during the whole time three or four sets of Nautch girls were singing, without a soul attending to them, the noise being far too great to hear, even had one wished it.

Coming home we managed to miss the General, and came through some other parts of the town, which were handsomer than the part we went through before ; though even in this so narrow that in one place we were near meeting with an accident by one's elephant being too high to pass under a brick archway, and we found, after crushing our cocked hats, that it would not do, and we were obliged to turn back after all.

We all dined with Captain Wade in the evening, at which two Seikh noblemen were present, and all Runjeet's French officers.

March 7th.—We marched out of Umritsir to a place about nine miles off, the residence of the bride's father, who is one of the oldest families in the Punjab, living in a large baronial-looking castle within sight of our present encampment.

At three we all started on elephants to make part of the procession towards the residence of the bride, and to see the distribution of (or rather scramble for) the money which the Maha Rajah throws on all sides, beginning with the pice, and ending, as he gets nearer the bride's residence, with gold ducats and mohurs.

The crowd assembled surpassed belief ; I should say it included from five to six hundred thousand persons, all shoving and fighting to get in one direction—near the Rajah's elephant. Several lives must have been lost from the crowd, and I myself saw one man knocked down by a mahout with the iron spike with which he drives the elephant, and the great brute trod upon him when down.

With a line of seventy elephants, and five or six hundred sewars (irregular horse), all of whom beat about them with huge sticks and the butt-ends of their carbines to clear the road, I do not think that we went at the rate of more than half a mile an hour.

Nowhere is that most wonderful of all created brutes shewn to so great an advantage as in a crowd like the present. In this instance, with the exception I have named, though hundreds were thrown under the feet of the elephants, and even in keeping their places many actually walked between the force and hind legs of the animals, still no one was touched ; and even when, as often happened, that it was impossible for the peolpe to get away from their feet, the animals would push them aside with their trunks, and, having thus cleared the way, move quietly and steadily on.

Long before the day was over, the crushing of the elephants one against the other, and the catching of the ladders hanging to their sides, had made sad work with our ghuls, or elephant saddle-cloths ; and some of those among the Seikhs, which must have been of great value from the richness of the embroidery, were, from their being less strong than English cloth, of which ours were made, torn literally to shreds and scattered to the winds.

After getting through the crowd, an almost equal difficulty

occurred in coming up to the steps by which we were to ascend into the house, and up to which only one elephant could come at a time ; so that, what with the crowd, the disagreeable smells, and heat, there was serious danger of being smothered before one had the least chance of getting upon the roof where the durbar was held.

After some shoving about and more noise I at last found myself under the canopy erected for the two chiefs, looking down on the main body of the building, covered with spectators, from the highest tower to the lowest court.

The bridgroom was now introduced for the first time, having his face covered with a veil made of strings of large pearls hung on gold thread. He is a thin, unhealthy-looking boy, dreadfully marked with the smallpox, but seemed intelligent and well-mannered. The brides (three in number) we do not see, of course. The religious parts of the ceremony were carried on in private, and finished at nine o'clock, which the Brahmins declare to be the propitious hours.

The crowd had diminished while we remained in the house, and we got away without much difficulty ; and after conducting the Maha Rajah home, went ourselves for an hour's rest, and then again started to witness the fire-works, let off on the occasion of the marriage, and to see a Nautch in the old chiefs tents.

We found him seatad, as usual, surrounded by his ministers and favourites, perched on a chair, with a highly embroidered gold stool for his knees to rest on. His dress was almost always the same (green Cashmere), and, with the exception of the rows of great pearls I beforc mentioned, and on state occasions the Kohe-noor, his great diamond, he very seldom wore jewels. He never was the cleanest person in the world, and his dress, I should imagine, was but seldom changed in any part. He has a curious habit of wearing but one stocking, from having had the rheumatism in one of his feet, which he thinks necessary to keep warm.

The whole time we remained a Nautch was going on, of which it was impossible to hear one syllable, every one talking as fast as possible. The Rajah sent round the intoxicating liquor which he drinks, at such a rate (particularly to the General, whose cup he always looked into to see that he really drank) that we were all right glad to get away, and retire to our beds, after one of the most fatigusing days I have ever experienced. The liquor he drinks would kill most people in a week, being, I should imagine, considerbly stronger than spirits of wine ; so much so as to bring tears into our eyes, even with the smallest quantity : and yet, during our different visits, he seldom drank less than several small glasses full, and without any apparent effect.

March 8th.—We made a useless march of three miles to pitch our camp nearer to his highness, to be more in the way of the general distribution of charity, when every person present receives one rupees as a mark of the liberality of the family. The manner of distributing money to such a multitude is rather curious, and an excellent expedient for preventing any one getting double allowance :—The whole crowd is driven into a space of about five miles in circumference, and entirely surrounded by soldiers, and out of this space no one is allowed to stir, except at eighty outlets, where as many officers are stationed distributing the money ; and as each one receives his rupee he is sent out of the circle, and not again allowed to enter.

They told us the number paid exceeded a million ; which, allowing *half* for Indian exaggeration, will leave five hundred thousand, which would probably be near the mark.

We did not see the distribution, but went instead to see the brides' dowry, consisting of 101 (considered as the lucky number) of every sort of animal, with the exception of elephants, which numbered but eleven. The horses, camels, and bullocks, were however there *bona fide,* and more than the number of other things. Some of the shawls, of which there were some 500 pairs, were most beautiful ; the jewels were many of them very handsome and of great iutrinsic value. Among other things was a complete set of native dinner and washing things, all of silver, and beautifully carved.

The Rajah insisted upon our again coming in the evening to see fireworks, which were much better than those of the previous night ; and, as we managed to escape finishing with a Nautch and drinking about, the evening passed off very pleasantly.

March 9th.—For the first time since we arrived at Amritsir we have had a whole holiday, and escaped without either Nautch or fireworks.

March 10th—Our march this morning was interrupted by our friend Sher Singh, who came to ask the Commander-in-chief to accompany him to see what he was pleased to call 'sport." We left the road and marched with a line of three elephants and 400 horsemen, for some time, without finding any thing ; at last a wretched hare took to her heels before us, and after running for some little way very quietly walked into a bush to avoid her enemies the hawks, which they had let loose at her, in addition to the said 400 gentlemen galloping and shouting ! As soon as they had watched her into the bush, the whole party surrounded it, and bringing out a great long net, deliberately set it where the poor devil must run. She managed, in spite of them, to get clear of thr bush, and nearly got away, till they rode over her and knocked her down with sticks. Altogether, I never saw a more deliberate murder. The chief's after-sport, which consisted in firing at doves and sparrows sitting, was not much better.

March 11th.—Our camp made a short move of three miles to a garden-house of Runjeet's two miles from the city of Lahore, where he is to give a grand *feteh* to our party either this evening or to-morrow, which depends on whether the water, which is brought from the Ravee (one of the five rivers from which the Punjab takes its name), has yet come sufficiently far down the canal which conducts it to this place, and which is necessary for the display of the fireworks.

It eventually turned out that we were not to have the entertainment till to-morrow, so that we shall have a day entirely to ourselves. We are to remain here till Monday, and then move about two miles nearer his place within the city.

March 12th.—A halt, the first we have had since leaving Meerutt, more than 300 miles to the southward, and, I believe, without the loss of a man. In the evening we all started on elephants to the Rajah's garden-house, about half a mile from the encampment, to see a display of fire and waterworks, given by Runjeet to the General; and to which, for the first time, the ladies, after much fighting, have been allowed to be *privately present.*

We found the whole place brilliantly illuminated with rows of small oil lamps, placed at regular intervals on the buildings and down the sides of the walks and tanks, which showed off the fountains to advantage: and at every ten or twelve yards coloured lamps were placed, to imitate branches of trees, festoons of flowers, &c.

From the open building where the court and ourselves sat, the whole scene looked more like an imitation of fairy-land at a theatre than any thing else, and at times I felt myself beginning to wonder when the spirits were going to appear.

All Runjeet's nautching, or dancing, arrangements are exercrable, as he allows the crowd to press in among the women as much as they please, entirely preventing their dancing; and the noise and talking going on the whole time prevent one's hearing one word of any of their songs, which (at no time the soul of harmony) are by this rendered unbearable.

The ladies of our party were stationed on the flat roof of the house, where a splendid tent was erected for their accommodation; thinking, I suppose, that *women* would be ashamed to show their faces to the gaze of the world at large. This not proving to be the case they had the prime-minister up to be introduced, and afterwards several of the Maha Rajah's court; and before they went away we had several of the prettiest Nautch girls to perform before them. As soon as the ladies had departed we again went into the audience hall, where the old lion was as usual plying the General with liquor and asking questions. The heat was getting disagreeable, and by nine o'clock we were all right glad to get away, after having seen altogether many sights that well repay whatever *disagreements* we may have experienced in arriving at them.

March 13*th.*—By Runjeet Singh's desire, we joined him on the march this morning near his garden-house, for the purpose of showing the General one of his country pavilions, and several small gardens which he has all along the road as resting-places from the hot winds. We supposed by his asking Sir Henry to accompany him this morning, and coming himself, with scarcely an attendant, that he intended to show the British chief to his people in his train, and wished us to ride with him through Lahore. But it proved afterwards that it was sheer good will and kindness to show him his flower-gardens, which are very gaily filled with stocks and poppies, and put one quite in mind of England with their scent. Runjeet Singh has no regular residence where he constantly lives, but instead is continually on the more, either in the wars in which he is constantly engaged, or moving from one part of his territory to another. For this purpose he has single rooms built along the lines of the great roads, so that in case the heat is too great for tents, a cooler place is always at hand.

We passed along the northern end of the city of Lahore, which has a very imposing effect, rising with its domes and minarets above the mass of cultivation by which it is surrounded. How any English farmer would have groaned if he had seen the dreadful waste of standing corn which we saw as we entered our camp, which was pitched in the centre of a plain, of 600 or 700 acres just coming into ear, great part of which was already cut down for the tents to stand on, and the remainder was rapidly undergoing the same fate, from camels, elephants, cows, and horses without number, being turned out to feed on it ! So much for an arbitrary and *military government* ! Whether taxes were remitted to these poor wretches who may have lost the entire produce of their year's labour we never learned, but at any rate no remission could have paid for their loss : but little money being among the lower classes of the country, and their food being thus destroyed, I much doubt if they had the means of purchasing elsewhere. The Seikhs never think of the cultivation on the march, driving their artillery carts and cavalry in every direction through the standing corn, if by that means they can save half a mile of ground, and laughing to scorn the efforts of the poor ryots (or cultivators) to save their devoted crops.

I spent tne evening in preparing a young horse of mine for his exaltation of the morrow, in being presented to the Maha Rajah (on his intended visit to the Commander-in-chief), as a specimen of the studs of the Hon. Company, having been purchased by government for that purpose.

March 14th.- Runjeet's official visit has, for reasons best known to himself, been postponed till the afternoon ; which allows one an extra hour or two's sleep- an enjoyment which we have had too little of lately to allow its being lightly thrown away.

A deputation, consisting of Colonels L. and C., Major F., and Captains W. and H., started at half-past three to conduct the

Maha Rajah to the camp, half way between which and his own the Genreal and the rest of his staff will meet him. He came, us usual, surrounded by his troops and courtiers ; and while passing through the escort, the whole of which was drwan up to reccive him, stopped three or four times and narrowly looked at the king's 13th and 16th Lencers, with which he always seems wonderfully delighted : these and the troops at Ronher (his meeting with Lord W. Bentinck on the Sutlej) being the only Europeans he has ever seen.

The durbar was arranged in the first tent, and the presents in the second. He never ceased asking questions from the moment he entered :- "What was the strength of the Indian army ?" "Did we think that Russian interest was doing us much harm in Persia ?" "Was it thought that Persia had sufficient power to give effectual aid to Russia in the event of their coming in this direction?" &c. &c. These and many other questions, put with the greatest acuteness, and many of them most difficult to answer, made that generally most dull of all amusements quite the reverse ; and though he remained far longer than is generally the case, none, I think, felt bored.

The General, after sitting more than an hour listening to and answering these questions, at last rose, and led the way to the rear tent, to show the Rajah his presents ; which consisted of one elephant, eight horses (mine among the number), a double-barrelled gun, rifle, and brace of pistols, and fifty-one pieces of different kinds of stuff, that number being the proper quantity for a crowned head. The General apologised that the presents were not better, saying that it was because he had not had sufficient warning of the honour he was about to receive, or that they should have been better. Runjeet Sing, previous to our visit to Lahore, had been so tenacious of the privilege of permitting persons to visit his country, that an invitation to so great a retinue as a

Commander-in-chief was certain to bring was quite unlooked for; and when it reached us, our time between receiving it and arrival at Lahore was far too short to provide such as Sir Henry would willingly have presented.

On his way out of the camp the Rajah had his elephant driven in among the guns, of which not the smallest matter seemed to escape his eye, questioning several of the drivers, and looking at the harness and equipment.

We all again conducted him half-way on his way home; and so long had he stayed, that it was nearly dark before the troops were all dismissed to their lines, and ourselves delivered from our red coats and embroidery.

March 15th.—We were all surprised this morning by the apparition of a strange-looking figure, in a flannel-jacket and trowsers, and straw hat, mounted on one of Runjeet's troop-horses, thoroughly beat, riding up to the tents; which turned out to be Mr. H., who has just arrived from Rajhmahl, in Lower Bengal, having had all manner of adventures. He travelled nearly 1,200 miles without stopping, passing through many a strange land, knowing but little of the language; and having, from the bearers in the Seikh's dominions being unaccustomed to their work, at last had his palanquin dropped in the road, to press broken-down troopers, ponies, and any other brutes he could get, to carry him on to his destination—our camp at Lahore. He had come by Sir Henry's invitation all this distance, simply to be present at these marriage ceremonies, for some of which he was too late, and having, after a very few days, to return whence he came.

He had not been to bed for thirteen days; but has, however, just arrived in time to wash and dress, and start with us to see some of Runjeet's irregular troops.

We found the old prince seated in one of his flower-gardens, with a road running through the centre, through which each horseman passed, presenting as he did so a nurzer, or a rupee or two, to each, according to his rank. The larger proportion of them were dressed in yellow silk, armed with matchlocks or spears, and tolerably mounted ; and if they did dot do much else they made a very splendid show. Some few were beautifully dressed in chain armour, and looked so like the pictures one sees of warriors in the time of Richard Coeur de Lion, that one might almost fancy one's self transported back to the time of the Crusaders ; for which all these gentlemen in yellow and all the colours of the rainbow, would make a good appearance as the soldiers of Saladin.

In this procession the Acalies, a sect of religious fanatics which Runjeet has vainly attempted entirely to disperse, did not take the least important or least curious part. Every extravagance that ever fakir or wild Irishman was guilty of, was here outdone. It is utterly indescribable, the dirt, rascality, and filth, which these brutes seem to glory in. Even in the presence of their master no one is safe ; and the chief himself shewed his doubts by ordering up a guard of regular troops, and placing the fanatics between two large bodies of cavalry. They are a sort of military madmen, sworn to defend the Hindoo religion ; but having at the same time a fancy for making irruptions into the Company's territories; which formerly was sufficiently disagreeable, but of late, from the severe way they were treated, both by their own government and ours, they have found that "discretion is the better part of valour." They make excellent soldiers individually, and the Rajah has taken great pains in so dispersing them among the different regiments as to prevent their fanaticism from becoming dangerous, which it is when they are in any number. Between 5,000 and 6,000 men marched past ; but so long were they about it, that, though we had started at four o'clock, it was nearly dark before it was over.

CHAPTER IX.

Grand Review of Runjeet's Troop—Extraordinary State of Discipline—Generals Ventura and Allard—M. Court—The Rajah's Delight at English Troops—Practice of English Artillery before the Rajah—The Rajah's Court Jewels—The "Mountain of Light"—Mode of gaining Possession of it—Treatment of Shah Suja—The Rajah's Fete in Honour of the Ladies—Presents—Give and Take—Strange. Scene between the Rajah and the Commander-in-Chief—Etiquette at Fault—A Native Chief—General Allard's Native Troops—Celebrated Steed and Sabre—Astrologer's Prediction—Visit of Leave-taking to the Rajah—Character of Runjeet Sing.

Marth 16*th*.—The first grand review of the whole of Runjcet's regulars assembled at Lahore. We found them, on coming to the ground, drawn up in line, extending two miles on the banks of the river, consisting of twenty-eight battalions of infantry and six of cavalry ; altogether about 18,000 men, exceedingly well clothed, and armed in the European fashion, with the exception of the cap, the aversion to which Runjeet has never been yet able entirely to overcome in his army : red turbans being substituted for the Shako, which I am not at all sure is not an improvement, for a more villanous head-dress thun the present shako never was invented.

On the right of the line was General Ventura's brigade, consisting of eight regiments of infantry, which he put through two movements, both of which they executed with equal steadiness and precision with our men. The General seemed much pleased at the Commander-in-chief's praise of his troops, the discipline of which is really wonderful, when one comes to consider the raw materials he has to work upon, and the prejudices he has to overcome.

Allard, Runjeet's oldest general, is just returned from France, and has not yet been replaced in his employment; and I should think would, if he could get his arrears of pay, leave Runjeet for France altogether.

These two officers, Generals Ventura and Allard, have been now, for many years, in the Maha Rajah's service, having come overland to him from Persia. To them, and to Monsieur Court, in the artillery branch of his service, he owes principally the really very advanced state of equipment and discipline to which his forces have been brought. The former is an infantry, the latter a French cavalry officer, having been at one time, I believe, aide-de-camp in Spain to Marshal Bessieres. Monsieur Court has brought his artillery and musketry to great perfection, the latter being quite as good as those of the Company, with the advantage of being lighter.

March 17*th.*—This morning Runjeet saw our escort, consisting of the squadrons of the 16th Lancers and 4th Cavalry, one troop of horse-artillery, 200 men of the 13th Light Infantry, and eight companies from the 18th, 20th and 17th regiments of Native Infantry. The extreme delight of the old man at the discipline of the men, and the explanation the General gave him of the movements, and how they would act with a large body, surpasses belief. He rode through and looked at every gun, examined the appointments of the men, counted the numders in each square, and quite gained all our hearts by the interest he took, and the acuteness which he shewed by his questions. After the review was over he begged the Commander-in-chief to allow him to send some mark of his bounty to the soldiers; and directly they got home he sent them 11,000 rupees, to be divided amongst them; which is a fine opportunity for all the Irishmen in the regiment to celebrate St. Patrick's day.

The Rajah said, among other things, that "His French officers and others had told him that English discipline was no thing; and that through so much was talked about it, still it was only outward show, and that where they came before an enemy the thing would bear a very different aspect. But *now*," he said, "I see what liars they are; you have shewn me, not only how troops can be moved, but also how those movements can be brought to bear upon a hostile force." He added, "that it was now no matter of wonder to him why the English had always been victorious in the East."

One of the movements that most delighted him, was the shewing how quickly a gun breaking down could be but together on the field, and be again on the march. It was ordered to be done by a six-pounder of one of the troops of horseartillery. It was thrown on the ground, dismounted from its carriage, taken all to pieces, remounted, men on their horses, and again in full gallop, in the space of five minutes. He could not, for some time, believe that it had really been taken to pieces, and would have it that they only stopped because some of the harness had been broken; and it had to be again performed before he could quite believe what he saw.

In the evening we saw more of the Rajah's irregular cavalry, the contingents of three Seikh chiefs. There were, also, some few Acalies; but neither so numerous nor so brutal-looking as before.

March 18th.—The Maha Rajah yesterday expessed a wish to see some artillery practice; accordingly, this morning we started te shew him the practice with grape, round-shot, and shrapnels. He had erected canvass targets, and the three first rounds of grape brought them both to the ground, with which he seemed delighted. They were again put up, and pierced through and through with shrapnels and case-shot.

Shere Sing, and many of the higher ranks of natives, dismounted from their horses, to watch the pointing of the guns, and see how it was done. At the end he stuck up his own chattah, or umbrella, and the fifth and sixth shots sent it to ribands, at 400 yards. Altogether, the whole thing was most successful, and shewed him a good specimen of what the British can do if called upon. So pleased was the old chief, that he has sent 1200 rupees additional to the artillery ; and to the officers who pointed the guns, a shawl and gold bangle each.

We went afterwards, by the Maha Rajah's invitation, to see the court jewwels, some of them the finest in the world They consisted of swords, armlets, hangles, necklaces and many others. The swords were many of them of very great value, their blades alone being, in some instances, valued at 1000*l*., and the gold and jewels upon their hilts and scabbards at five times that sum. Many of them had been squeezed out of Shah Suja, the ex-king of Caboul, when he took refuge in Runjeet's dominions, after his expulsion from his own. They were mostly in velvet scabbards, richly embroidered in gold, the clasps, hilt, and points being of massy metal, covered with precious stones.

The most valuable and greatest sight, however, was the great diamond (I believe the largest but one in the world), called the Koh-e-noor, or Mountain of Light, valued at three millions and a half of money. It is badly cut, and very plainly set in gold:

and did one not know its value, one would have set it down as a bad lustre.

The manner in which Runjeet obtained this and the other valuables of the Affghan monarch were highly characteristic of an Eastern despot. For some time after the Shah's arrival at Lahore he was treated with great distinction, and promised aid to recover his throne. But this soon changed, and first persuasions, and at length threats were used, to induce him to give up his jewels, without success. At last, finding every other plan fail, the royal family were at first straightened in quantity, and at length kept entirely without food, till these jewels (the principal part of the fortune he had brought with him from Affghanistan) were delivered over to Runjeet.

Even after the delivery of his wealth the Shah was not allowed to rest in peace; insult followed insult, until at length he contrived first to get his family conveyed away, and lastly he himself effected his, by climbing over the roofs of houses, and under the walls of the city by a sewer, out of the city of Lahore, and took refuge in the British dominions; where he has since resided, entirely living on a pension assigned to him by the Company.

March 19th.—This morning we saw General Ventura's brigade of regular troops, consisting of three regiments of infantry and ten pieces of artillery. They changed position several times, but have little idea beyond remaining steady in line to perfection.

In the evening we all went to the palace, to be present at a grand entertainment given by Runjeet to the ladies. The palace we had seen before, on going to see the great diamond and other jewels. The room the entertainment was given in was fitted up all round with small mirrors, fixed in the wall with enamel, which shone like diamonds in candlelight, and had a very beautiful effect. Nautching, drinking, and fireworks, were, as usual, the order of the day : which, to many, is very tiresome ; but to me, who am fond of a Nautch, it is not disagreeable.

Nautching requires, like many other things, to be accustomed to before liking it. When we first went to India, our party, without exception, noted it the most atrocious screaming they were ever condemned to hear ; but they each and ali gradually began to look upon it as less disagreeable, and towards the end of our stay even thought it, in many instances, rather pleasant than otherwise. Many of the airs are simple and sweet ; but too often their effect is spoiled by the screaming which most of the singers think it necessary to make, the natives prefeerring the louder to the sweeter melody; and that Nautch girl who can make most noise being generally looked upon as the prima donna.

March 20th.—The ladies all went in the afternoon to see Runjeet's wives. They found the oldman himself seated in the midst of them, who talked with them for some time, and afterwards gave them some very handsome presents, which I hope they may be allowed to keep.

This remark arises from an excellent, but still, at times, most vexatious rule, of our government, which positively forbids any European in their service from keeping their presents received from natives. This at first sounds harsh : but it must be remembered that, under the name of presents, bribes may and have been given ; and also, that as natives always expect, in return for the presents they give, that an equivalent should at all times be given, the Company have, therefore, taken upon themselves both the give and take : for though most of us will gladly receive those articles usually given by natives, the greater part of them being no earthly use to us, we shold look very black at having to give, out of our own pockets, an equivalent for nominal value received. The Government therefore, order their political agents to give presents in your own name, and to receive those offered in return: the latter to be sold for the benefit of government.

The General and myself went over the river to see the tomb of Shah Jehan—a most beautiful building, the tomb itself inlaid like the Taj, but dreadfully out of repair; as Runjeet, whenever he wants stone fot any purpose, pulls down part of this without the slightest compunction. The water was just deep enough to prevent our going across on our elephants, and they were accordingly made to swim over, while were ferried across in a boat. It is a dangerous amusement going over a river in a howdah, for the elephant, if he finds the thing in any degree too heavy, often shakes, or even pulls it off, and a very unpleasant ducking, or even drowning sometimes follows.

March 21*st*.—A visit, in the afternoon, to Kurruck Singh, the eldest and least interesting of the whole family. He received the General in one of his father's flower-gardens outside of the city, and gave himself great airs, not even coming part of the way to meet our chief. He looks as if he smoked day and night, and had smoked away the whole of his intellects. I take his party to be the smallest of the whole three which are likely to divide the Punjab at Runjeet's death; and that were it not for his son, who seems a much more intelligent person than his father, his chance of succession (even with the treasure which Runjeet will probably leave him) would not be worth much.

March 22*nd*—To-day begins the Seikh festival of the Holi, or rejoicing at the commencement of spring. The Rajah expressed a wish that the General would come, and be present at part of the ceremoney at his tents. He accordingly went, accompanied only by us of the *personal* staff; and a most extraordinary scene it was. We found him seated, surrounded, as usual, by his court and the firsr time, the guard of Amazons, some thirty or forty in number, many of them very pretty, armed with bows and arrows, which they drew the moment we made our appearance, in the most warlike style. This corps is one formed of ladies, and which has been often previously mentioned in other works on India, but till this occasion they never made their appearance in our presence. Whether in presence of an enemy they would be found equally bold, I know not, but in that of the old chieftain they dared to do and say in a way that none of his most favourite courtiers ventured to attempt.

In front of every chair were small baskets, heaped one above another, full of small, brittle balls, filled with red powder, and alongside them large bowls of thick yellow saffron, and long gold squirts, with which each of us armed ourselves. As soon as we were all seated, the Rajah took a large butter-boat kind of article, filled with the said saffron, and poured it on Sir Henry's bald head; while, at the same time, the prime minister rubbed him over with gold and silver leaf, mixed with red powder.

We were all holding our side with laughter at the chief bowing to all this, wondering the meaning of it, when our mirth (or rather mine) was changed into grief at having one eye nearly put out by a long-bearded gentleman opposite, who deliberately threw a ball, filled with red powder, into one eye, while another factious youth closed up the other with saffron soup. The origin of this ceremony I am not sufficiently acquainted with Hindoo mythology to explain, but the custom of throwing red powder about is universal among that sect througout India; and our servants, though prevented by respect from actually committing the atrocity, still bring round a plate with some of it at this season, and expect a present in return.

Runjeet himself seemed to enjoy the fun as much as any one; and though few of the courtiers aimed at him personally, this did not prevent his taking an occasional shot himself, his being more particularly directed against an Affghan ambassador, just arrived at his court from Candahar.

This poor man was dressed in his best, his beard combed and died to a nicely, his feet tucked well under him, and his face drilled to a grave, diplomatic caste.

Never having before seen the festival of the Holi, he had not the smallest idea what he had to expect, and his look of astonishment of a ball of red dust being shyed in his eye, and his horror when his beard was turned to a bright saffron colour, I shall long remember. This soon turned all our ammunition upon him, and first one eye and then another was closed up, till at length he was fairly beat out of his etiquette, and took his heels amidst a roar of laughter from all our party.

The battle raged for more than an hour, during which neithor the Commander-in-chief nor the Amazons came off scot free ; and by the time we all got up to return home, the honourable company of London chimney-sweeps would have turned us out as too dirty for their society.

March 23rd.—The second day of the festival we have managed to escape ; and only those who are fools enough to go of their own accord, get their clothes spoiled and their eyes closed up; and, for the first day since we arrived at Lahore, this has passed without any procession or show.

March 24 th.—After the usual morning review of some of Runjeet's regulars, which they call the French brigade, but which seem the only ones that can move at all, and these not much. we went in the afternonn to pay u visit, in company with the Maha Rajah, to him of Nabur, a feudatory of Runjeet's on our side of the Sutlej. He is a very old man of seventy, with a venerable white beard, and received us in a very good durbar, in the court-yard of the Motee Musjid, the principal ancient mosque at Lahore; which looked very picturesque, with its domes appearing over the crimson tents, and handsomely dressed natives in the durbar. He presented six or seven horses, and some very handsome shawls; all of which were, however, sent back afterwards.

March 25th.—We had out this morning three regiments of cavalry, under the French general Allard, both of whom (the troops and Allard) made a most horrible exhibition, making a farce of the whole thing. In the afternoon, Runjeet invited us to come and see a review of 1,100 Affghan, just come over to him from Dost Mahommed, under the command of Pere Mahommed Khan, whom he has prevailed upon, partly by fear and partly by bribes, and whose defection is like to lead to that of his elder brother, who is still with the Cabul chief; in which case the cause of Dost Mahommed is likely to go to the dogs. His men are the wildest and most soldier-like looking we have yet seen, all dressed in chain armour, with large jack boots, armed with spears, and looking more like Cossacks than any thing else.

Among other presenis, these Affghans brought to the Rajah a celebrated horse, called the "Mountain of Light," which he has for years been trying to get, hitherto without success; they also brought a celebrated Khorassan sabre, valued at 10,000 rupees,. These chiefs had had charge of the valley of Peshawer for the Affghans, and Runjeet having now conquered country they have, either from fear of returning to their own country, or thinking that the Rajah's service was likely to be more profitable, delivered themselves into his power, and received grants of land within the Seikh dominions.

During the time they were marching past, the General and Runjeet were in deep consultation relative to the trade of the Indus, which they have at length arranged, much to the satisfaction of both parties. Runjeet is to send, immediately, seven merchants, in company with a European officer (Mr. Mackinson), with goods, in salt and shawls, to the value of a lac of rupees, towards

Bombay, by way of the Indus, of which Runjeet has a considerable share himself. This expedition, should it prove profitable, will, it is hoped, lead to the open navigation of the Indus, and great increase to our trade in that quarter.

At this interview, Runjeet told the Commander-in-chief that the astrologers had found that the planets would not be propitions to our going on the 27th. and he consequently hoped we would defer our departure till the following day, which they had fixed upon as being more so. The General was obliged to do this, though much against his will, as the season will even now be so far advanced before the European troops can again reach their quarters, that even the delay of a single day is not to be lightly passed over.

March 26th.—Passed in entire peace and quietness, which the exception of a dinner-party at night to different people in the camp.

March 27th.—At four we all started to pay our last and farewell visit to the old Rajah, previous to our departure of tomorrow. We found him seated in his garden-house, with tame pigeons feeding on the carpet before him, and even a larger court than usual in attendance.

While we were at Lahore, the Rajah seldom received us at the palace, preferring (what was much more convenient for us) to hold his durbar in one or other of the many garden-houses he has round the city. They generally consist of one or two small rooms only, with a small level piece of ground outside, on which is spreuad the carpets, and chairs placed in a circle on them. On ordinary days his son, his prime-minister, and one or two others, form, with servants, his party. Three or four children, generally sons of his old servants, who have been killed in his service, scramble about the carpet with the tame pigeons; half-a-dozen favourite horses, reined up and fat as hogs, march about in front ; while the few guards and attendants shew the confidence the old man in his people and in those around him.

The first half hour was spent in civil speeches between the two great men, and expressions of friendship which it was hoped would always exist between their respective governments. After this had gone on for some time, the farewell presents were brought, which to the General were most magnificent, in shawls, a most beautiful sabre, elephants, and horses ; and afterwards something was brought to every body in succession.

My share of the presents was a pretty cloak enough, and a pair of gold bangles, which I must own rather disappointed me in my expectations. But this was splendid in comparison with some, who merely got a dirty old matchlock, worth five or six rupees ; the Seikhs knowing so well that all goes into the Company's hands, that handsome presents are now no longer given.

After every one had got something, the General rose to bid adieu : and I am sure both him and almost every one present felt sincere sorrow at parting from the good-natured, kind old man, whom we had all begun to consider as an old friend, and to treat accordingly. He shook each of us by the hand, and gave the Commandhr-in chief and his military Secretary a new order, which he is instituting on the plan of the Legion d'Honneur of France.

Runjeet, among his subjects, has the character generally of a kind and generous master, and one of the best princes that has ever reigned in India. As evidence of his being a really good and amiable man, may be cited his kindness to children (two or three of whom he has crawling about the durbar), and the fact of his never having, since he conquered the country, put a man to death for even the most heinous crimes. His exceeding kindness and good nature throughout our entire visit, to all in any way attached to us, makes us believe that such is his real character. At all events it is certain, that, without the punishment of deat, this chief yet manages to keep his wild people in perfect subjection, substituting an occasional cutting off of noses and ears, and more often a sound bastinadoing ; by which means his country is kept in perfect order, his revenue duly paid, and he himself supposed to have collected an enormous treasure*

*Since writing the above, great changes have taken place among the Seikh chiefs here spoken of. Runjeet Sing is himself no more ; Kurruck Sing, his eldest son, is also dead ; and the grandson, whose marriage we came to celebrate, succeeded to the throne, not without considerable suspicion of having caused his father's death. He again, in his turn, has been killed by a beam falling on his head in gateway; on which the widow of Kurruch Sing seized the reins of government, which she continues to hold, assisted by Runjeet's prime-minister, Dhian Singh.

CHAPTER X.

Departure from Lahore—Splendid Ruins—Frightful death—Celebrated Fort—Trait of Character—Alarming News—Three Tigers—Crossing the Sutlej—Home Association—The Himalayah Mountains—Pinjore—Beautiful Gardens of the Rajah—Reception of the Commander-in-chief—Travelling in the Hills—Beauty and Fashion of Subattoo—Native Troops Attacking a Stockade—Arrival at Simlah—Description of Simlah—Its Superb Situation—the Rainy Season.

March 28th.—Left Lahore, passing under the walls of the town, and marched ten miles, chiefly through ruins of the ancient capital, which, in the time of the Mogul emperores, must have rivalled Delhi and Agra themselves in extent. Lahore was formerly the capital of India, previous to the Mahommedan conquerors settling themselves at Agra and Delhi ; and in those times was celebrated for its great size and magnificence, both now depated from it. Its modern grandeur (of which the ruins of some few fine buildings still remain to shew that it once existed) it owes to the Emperor Humaioon, who established his capital here for some years, and made it his favourise residence.

March 29th.—The desolate state of this part of the country, and want of water, have given us a most awful march this morniug of nearly twenty miles, which obliged the General to serd on ail the infantry at three o'clock in the morning, so as to get in by eight o'clock. The whole country we passed through seemed to have been once cultivated in the prosperous days of the Mogul empire, but for many years to have been now let to grow to jungle.

March 30*th*.—Poor T., ae ensign in the 18th N. I.. who has been some days ill with the small-pox, died last night. Any thing more horrible than this mode of death cannot be conceived,- every body afraid to come near him, even in his last moments ; and then to be shovelled into the earth, and left in the midst of strangers, both to his religion and his country !

We rode through the town of Kussoor, under which we are encamped, which is celebrated for the number of asseults it stood against Runjeet's best troops, and his being unable at last to take it, except by treachery. It is the principal place of manufacture in his dominions for the ornamental-work on leather. in saddles, bridles, and shoes, which the Seikhs admire so much.

As we were coming back we heard the firing over poor T., and on riding up to the place, Shere Sing who was with the Genral, gained all our hearts, by dismounting and strewing flowers over his grave' in addition to giving orders that a guard should be placed over it until a wall could be built round. It is a great comfort to think that the poor fellow's resting-place will be respected.

This place, like te preceding, must, in its time, have been very extensive, the ruins extending for miles in every direction.

March 31*st*. – To-day's march again brought us to the banks of the Sutlej, and tosmorrow will see us out of Runjeet's territories. The Genral had a durbar in the evening, for the audience of departure to Shere Sing. We all were really sorry to part with him, and made him a present of one of his own guns, together with a buggy and horse, with which he seemed delighted.

News has been sent of three tigers being in this immediate neighbourhood, in an island in the river. This information immediately collected a large party for tomorrow morning, who, however, failed in finding any thing beyond the marks of the animals.

April 1st.—Saturday. We recrossed the Sutlej, about five miles from the twon of Feeroozpoor, without the loss of any thing belonging to the camp. with the exception of one boatman, who perished by his own boat going down. The river at this place is considerably wider than where we crossed before (probably 600 yards), with the same kind of barren country on either side.

The town of Feeroozpoor, under which we are encamped, has just fallen to our government, as lords paramount, by the death of an old woman, to whom it belonged, and is now undergoing many impovements, to fit it as a proper depot for our *expected* trade on the Sutlej and Indus ; for which its situation, so near to the Maha Rajah's town of Kussoor, and to Lahore itself, admirably fits it.

April 2nd.—Sunday. Halt ; and ride round the city in the evening, during which we had a heavy storm of rain, and got thoroughly wet ; which, I hope, will carry us on tolerably cool to the hills.

April 8th.—For the last six days we have continued our march regularly towards the hills, which we now begin to look forward to, as the heat begins to be much felt by us all.

April 12th.—The character of the appearance of this part of the country is totally changed from what we are accustomed to, most of the fields being so completely enclosed, that on the march this morning, after leaping a small fence into one of the fields, I found myself thoroughly pounded, as my horse would not again cross the fence he had already come over, and by no means relished charging the one in his front. It ended by my nearly getting a fall, from his rushing through a thick fence, with a straw rope run alonge it, over which he fell. Enclosures in India there are none, except just in this part ; and were it not for the rivers and water-courses, one might ride from one end of the country to another without a chance of being stopped by a fence. The divisions of the fields are marked by small aidges of earth, and the rights of the different proprietors are perfectly understood by this simple means.

The villages for the most part are strong and flourishing, and more cultivation about them than in any of the protected Seikh states we have hitherto passed through, the Rajah of Patialah, to whom the country generally belongs, having an excellent character among his people. In the afternoon some of our party rode through a country that put us all in mind of home, and the green laness smelling of wild-flowers most deliciously.

April 13*th.*—A very long march, of sixteen and a half miles, to Nandpoor Kalawar, through much of the same kind of country as yesterday. We found our halting-place pitched under the walls of a small, but prettily situated mud fort, kept up by the Patialah Rajah, with the mountains in its rear. The Himalayah mountains look magnificent from its walls, which also command a very charming view over the beautifully wooded and cultivated country of the Tirai.

April 16*th.*—Arrived at Monai-Majrah, the Rajah of which, a dependant to him of Patialah, met the General five miles from the camp ; which is rather a singular fact, as getting tipsy is said to be "his custom always in the afternoon." I have made a sketch of his place and part of the village surrounding it, with a distant view of the Himalayah mountains, towards Rouper.

The mountains look most beautiful from this place, and make one quite long to be in them.

April 17th.—Pinjore. The gardens of this place are celebrated all through India for their water-works, which were made by the Mogul emperors for one of their hot-weather residences, and were given up to the Rajah of Patialah by our government after the Goorcah war. The Rajah had sent a Vakeil and Nautch girls for the General's amusement, who performed before us, after seeing the fireworks in the gerdens, which were very indifferent.

April 18th.—Marched to Bahr, where we leave all our tents, horses, &c., and tomorrow commence the ascent to Subattoo. From this the road which we see on the side of the mountain looks nearly perpendicular, and much more grand than beautiful, as the mountains are almost entirely without verdure, or trees of any kind, and by no means come up to the glowing descriptions given us by travellers.

A short ride which myself and some others of the party took this evening, over part of to-morrows's journey, did not turn out so awful as we expected ; and, with the exception of some of our party, all threaten to become tolerable hill-travellers.

April 19th.—I took leave of my tents and marching equipage with regret ; for taking them altogether, the seven months that we have been on the move have been both the most eventful and perhaps the happiest part of my life, and I much doubt if Simlah will be found so agreeable as our camp-life has proved.

Our long march of fifteen miles was rendered double by the continual (almost perpendicular) ascents and descents which e had to-day between Bahr and Subattoo ; and particularly the last part into that cantonment was about the longest and steepest pull I ever had, and afforded a good chance of breaking one's neck.

Subattoo itself, when once arrived at, was a very curious and pretty little plain in the centre of a magnificent amphitheatre of hills, rising one above another on every side. It is about 5,000 feet above the level of the sea ; and yet, even at this great height, is not quite free from the hot winds, which are at times felt severely,

We rode in the evening with the commandant and political agent for this part of the Company's territory (commanding also the Goorcah battalion, stationed at this place), to see a stockade which his men are to storm to-morrow. It was perched on the brow of a hill, with precipices on either side, and was by no means a place which one would pick out for one's morning's amusement to attack in earnest.

This Goorcah battalion is one of the many raised by the Company for the protection of particular portion of their territory. The men of this corps are Goorcahs, or mountaineers, from the Nepaul hills. They are very short, yet strong and active fellows, brave to a proverb, and eminently formed for the work they have to do. Recruiting is now grown difficult, from obstructions thrown in their way by the Nepaul government ; and some a different caste have of late been permitted to enter the corps.

In the evening we all dined with the Colonel, and met all the beauty and fashion of Subattoo, consisting of two ladies and four of the other sex.

April 20th.—The Goorcah battalion paraded this morning for Sir Henry's inspection. They are dressed and look personally very much the same style of men as the Ceylon corps, though I should say they are very inferior in equipment, having muskets in place of rifles, and their clothes but very indifferently made. They were, however, in exceedingly good order, and marched past as well as any regiment could do. In the afternoon they attacked the stockade; four companies defending and the same number attacking, with the remainder forming the reserve. It made a very pretty show; the little fellows cutting down the stockade with the talwars (a small kind of sword), which is their national weapon, and driving the defenders out in capital style.

April 21st.—We started at day-light, mountain ponies having been substituted for our Arabs, and travelled over some tolerably precipitous roads to Cyrey, a half-way house between Simlah and Subattoo; one of the coldest, bleakest, and most miserable looking places I ever saw, with two wretched rooms without fire-places. We managed, however, to pass the day very comfortably, and in the evening went on to Simlah; which, I think, we all agreed was about the only thing in India we had not been disappointed in.

The mountain roads, though perheps made too much on the General Wade principle, of straight up one hill and down the other side, are nevertheless excellent in their way, particularly immediately around the station; and after a few days' practice in the hills the most timid person gets thoroughly accustomed to them. No carriage has ever yet made its way to Simlah, the roads being too narrow to admit of more than one, which would of itself fill up the entire width; and should a second meet it, either one or the other must of necessity go down the precipice.

For the last three miles before coming to the station, the whole of the hills were covered with ilex and rhododendron trees, the latter in the most magnificent scarlet flower I ever beheld, and growing, not as in England, a miserable shrub, but as a tree of some size.

This mountain station has now been for many years established, and every succeeding year proves its advantages and adds to its popularity. It is something more than 7,000 feet above the level of the sea, and, with the exception of the rainy season, which begins about the middle of June and ends early in September, a more delicious climate cannot be. During the rains it is. bowever, detestable from the clouds, which are continually walking into one's house, and the dampness which they create on every thing around. But even at this season it seldom happens that one is not able to get a ride or walk at some hour or other of the day.

The houses are built on a high ridge of mountains running east and west, terminated by a mountain called Jako, covered with timber, and now also built upon in every place where a wall could possible stand. Ronnd this mountain is the principal ride at Simlah, nearly seven miles long, hardish for horses' legs, but otherwise excellent, both as regards scenery and the safety and excellence of the road. From the houses on the main ridge the views are superb. The ranges of mountains rise one above another, till at length the snowy range, some 24,000 feet above the sea, forms a splendid termination of the prospect on that side ; while below, a gradual descent and successive ranges of smaller hills at length sink into the plains, through which on clear days, the Sutlej and Ganges may be seen to wind.

My chief's house is perhaps the best in Simlah ; it is beautifully situated on this ridge, and was built for the late Governor-General, Lord Willam Bentinck. Houses generally here let very high, and to a person resident on the spot, who can see them properly attended to, are excellent property ; but without this, the climate is such that a year or two of neglect soon destroys the best of them.

The sameness of our lives here, unless I made an expedition into the interior, will make it not worth while to continue my journal till we again descend into the plains. I shall therefore shut the book until that event occurs.

July 6th.—The rains commenced on the 6th of July, nearly a month later than ordinary. This circumstance has caused considerable distress among the peasantry, from the probable failure of their rice crops. Now that they have commenced they are, however, in earnest; and St. Swithin seems to have visited Simlah for his health: the rain coming down more as if it was poured out of a large bucket than in any other mode. Rain in Europe, and "the rains" of India, are very different things; and to a person unacquainted with the latter, it seems marvellous how one manages not to be washed away, house and home. For between two and three months it scarcely ever stops, night or day, and the quantity of water that falls in so short a time is almost past belief.

August 16th.—We experienced to-day a very severe shock of an earthquake, the first I ever felt. The shock in my house was very perceptible, making the beams of my room crack, and shaking down a bottle which was standing on the chimney-piece; above, it stopped the clock; and in many parts of Simlah frightened the good people so much as to make them run out of their houses in fear and trembling, lest they should fall on their heads. It happened at a quarter to one, and did not last more than three or four seconds.

The sketch on the opposite page is the jompawn used by

the Europeans in the hills, and is by far the safest mode of conveyance in them ; as the bearers are so sure-footed than an accident, even in the most difficult passes of the Himalayah, was never known to happen. Four is the number who actually carry the article, but most people have at least eight, for relays.

CHAPTER XI.

Expedition to Kotghur—Travelling in the Himalayah—Enormous Pines—Habits of the Hill-Carriers—Scarcity of Water—Impracticable Road—Native Chief—Arrival at Kotghur—The Snowy Range of the Himalaya—Agriculture in the Mountains—A Contumacious Deity—Extreme Cold of the Nights—Partridges—A Bad Shot—Return to Simlah.

THE difference in the temperature, and charge from hard and regular exercise to the sedantry life one leads here, has so much affected both Sir H.'s and my own health, that change of air is prescribed for us; and consequently the former determined to start, taking myself and two others of his staff with him, on an expedition to Kotghur, a small hill-station to the north of Simlah.

September 23th.—Started at day-light, or soon after, to overtake the General, who had already started on his way to Fargoo, the first-stage bungalow *en route* to Kotghur; overtook him just beyond Mahassoo, the scene of the Simlah pick-nicks, the nearest and most beautiful ridge of mountains between Simlah and the snowy range; and marched with him to the bungalow placed on a ridge above the road, thirteen miles from Simlah, and about 9,500 feet above the level of the sea. The house itself is in no way remarkable, though the scenery of the ridge on which it stands is particularly fine, and its timber the largest I have seen in the hills. We examined a pine on a former expedition to Mahassoo, which measured at two feet from the ground 19 feet in circumference; and though this was a large specimen, there were to be seen there many nearly as large.

Our party, consisting of Col. B. the military Secretary, Captain H. the Persian interpreter, and the General, remained stationary the remainder of the day, and at night we betook ourselves to the tents (of which we have three large ones), and his Excellency to the warm and smoky room of the bungalow.

Almost every thing in an expedition like the present, in the Himalayahs, has to be carried on men's shoulders; great numbers of men being employed in this way. Our tents, cooking utensils, baggage of all kinds, and, in short, every thing we had, moved in this way,—from 200 to 300 men being thus employed. They will go almost any distance in this way if one only pays them accordingly, and, when that is done, no hill seems too long for them, no valley too steep. They have no clothes to encumber them, which one is surprised at in this cold country. In the plains of India a man's wardrobe is not extensive, but here it is still so; in fact, with the exception of a very small rag, they wear none at all. When they can afford it, however, no people are better or more comfortably dressed. Their clothes then consist of a long kind of frock-coat, with large sleeves, trousers wide and thick, and a very neat small cap on their heads. Most of them are particularly muscular and well-made men, more especially about the legs, where many might be taken as models for a statuary. The continually ascending mountains bring these muscles into play, and their limbs have the appearance of the strength of the elephant. All the larger goods, such as tents, boxes, &c. &c., are carried on their shoulders, slung to poles; while the smaller, such as kettles, cooking utensil, &c., are placed in baskets made on purpose, and carried on their backs.

September 24th.--We mounted our ponies at day-light, and moved forward one half the way towards our encampment for the night, which will be at Mutteeana. We found our advaneed tents pitched within 100 yards of the magnificent road, soon after finishing the ascent of an enormous mountain, one of the most precipitous we have yet had on this expedition.

The only fault to be found with our mid-day encampment was its want of water, which very necessary article was fetched from a distance of two hours' travel by the bheestys, or water-carriers for each mussuc, a leather bag for water.

In the afternoon we continued our journey to the bungalow of Mutteeana, a tolerate room, but more cheerful than the dog-hole of yesterday. These bungalows have been built, at the expense of government, on all the great roads throughout India, for the benefit of travellers; and even in this out-of-the-way country they have not been forgotten, a small charge of a rupee being levied on every one using them. Tea, as usual, concluded the day; and with the exeption of a snoring servant. whose nose kept me awake the whole night, we finished the evening without adveuture.

September 25th.—Started at the usual bour from Mutteeana to march to a place laid down for our encampment. Our route passed an enormous ravine near the village of Kuljain, by a descent hearly perpendicular, and an ascent on the other side equally severe. After the ascent the road led along a ridge of hills for some distance, intersected by several streams and platos, wich would answer for an excellent encampment at any time. The latter part of the road between the village of Mutteeana and that of Jimmoo, where the advanced tents were pitched, was the worst of this line; and the ground when we arrived was not good, and was not improved by a heavy strom of rain, which fell in great quantities for two hours.

We again started after dinner for Nurkunda, the rain having rendered the roads between our last encampment and the bungalow so slippery in many parts as to be nearly impassable at the very steep pitches, of which there were many. Almost the entire road between Jimmoo and the Nurkunda bangalow was one steep ascent, running through some very wild and beautiful scenery, up to the Huttoo ridge, on which the house is built. A few yards from the bungalow the general was met by the Rana of Kumaisen, a petty sovereign af a considerable number of barren hills round Kotghur, with a revenue of about 8000 rupees annually (800*l.*), for which he pays a trifling tribute in money to Company. He brought a nurzer (or present) of a fowl. honey, and vegetables, and numerous civil speeches. He seemed a respectable old man, without any thing remarkable about him in anr way,

Sir Henry and the Chief talked over the state of the country, &c., and after staying about half-an-hour he took his departure.

The bungalow proved a very good one, of one large and two small rooms, with excellent verandahs on all sides. The old chieftain was very civil in supplying all the horses with forage and straw, which saved a world of trouble ; and the night passed more comfortably, and with less noise, than any has yet done since we started.

September 26th.—Sir Henry having passed a bad night, and not feeling well, desired B. and myself to proceed, while he remained with Captain H. to follow in the course of the day. The March was almost entirely on a descent. For the first time I saw the horse-chestnut and sycamore, both growing with great luxuriance and even to some size, and the pines where some of them nearly as large as those at Mahassoo.

During the march we descended more than 3000 feet, which at length took us to the of Kotghur, beautifully situated 6900 feet above the level of the sea, on the side of a partially wooded mountain, at the foot of which runs the sutlej. Kotghur was formerly the station of two companies of Sepoys, who were stationed here to defend this extreme out work of the Company's diminion. This station was abandoned in 1830, leaving merely a small guard of the Goorcah battalion, who are relieved every two months, and the bungalows belonging to the officers who had been quartered at the place. These latter now form a very convenient spot as a resting-place in a little expedition like the present. The honse we are in is an excellent one, holding the whole of our party with ease, and would, if kept in repair, be one of the best in the hills.

The General arrived about four o'clock, in time for dinner, and found every thing so comfortable as to make him determine to remain here to-morrow, and ttrn home-wards on the following day.

September 27ih.—We remained quietly in the house the whole of this, our day of rest, excepting a short agricultural ride after dinnet, followed by half the population of the place. The lands are let by the Company in leases of five years ; the first three of new lands being broken up, being allowed to them withot rent, to induce more cultivation. This mode of proceeding answers well, and the cultivation is yearly on the increase.

The Sutlej, at the foot of the hill on which the cantonment stands, is the boundary of our empire ; Runjeets dominions being immediately on the opposite bank, in the district Cooloo, one of his tributaries.

Septembr 28th.—Early in the morning we quitted Kotghur and arrived again at Nurkunda to breakfast, making the journey in three hours and twenty-five minutes. Our way lay through the most beautiful forest scenery we have perhaps yet met with, and which was seen to better advantage returning than it had it had been in going to Kotghur. The journey was altogether most severe for our horses, from being one continued ascent. We mounted during the ride more than 3,000 feet.

For the first time since our journey we had a superb view of the snowy range from the bungalow, which is seen from it to great advantage, the ridge on which the house is placed being higher than any of the intermediate ones between them and it, and consequently giving a view of the whole amphitheatre of eternal snow.

September 29th.—On starting in the morning the weather looked threatening and disagreeable, and before we had got over half our journey, heavy storms of rain, with thunder and lightning, came on, and made our tents when we arrived as disagreeable and uncomfortable as could well be. The rain ceased towards the afternoon, and the General was for going to see the house of one of the hill chieftains (he of Kumaisen's), which was perched upon a ridge of barren hills, about a mile from the place of encampment. But on demanding of the chief man of the village whether there would be any objection to such a proceeding, we were told that a very powerful god resided in one part of the building, and that he would be greatly offended at the intrusion of any person but a true believer in his godship ! So the plan was consequently abandoned.

In the evening we again ensconced ourselves in the Mutteeana bungalow ; and, with the exception of the cold, which was awful in my tent, which let in every breeze from the top of the hill, the night passed in comfort.

September 30*th*.—Our advanced tents had been sent on over-night to Theog, an old Goorcah fort, to be pitched under the hill on which stand the ruins of the old fortress of that name, now deserted. From the quantity of partridges we had seen on our way to Kotghur, we had hoped to have a day's shooting at this place ; but a mistake which the General made in the day of our arrival baffled this project, and the guns had not arrived when we did This was the more unlucky, as when we arrived within 200 yards of the tents we spied a large covey of fourteen, sitting in some stubble close to the side of the road. An old shikaree (or hunter), however, who was with us, armed with a rusty matchlock, was despatched to have a pot-shot at them. He accordingly sneaked round the field until, with the aid of a bush which stood between him and them, he got within ten yards, aimed right in the centre of them as they sat, put his light to the touchhole, fired, and missed !

After this exploit we proceeded on to our tents, where we remained till the evening, and then finished our day's work at our old smoky quarter of Fargoo.

October 1*st*.—The first day of the month, the last we have to stay in the hills, opened with the coldest morning I have yet seen in India. The thermometer stood, when we took our departure from the rest-house, at 38°, only six degrees above freezing, with an air bracing in proportion. I accordingly dismounted at the top of the hill, and walked the remainder of the way to the half-way house between Simlah and Mahassoo, where our tents were placed.

As usual, we remained in the tents during the heat of the day, and at four once more began our march home ; which was more welcome than I thought I should have felt it after so pleasant a trip

The Simlah season, like that of London, consists in a certain number of months, always at the same time of the years, namely, from May until October, being the time at which the climate of the plains of Upper India is more particularly distressing.

During the latter month a general break-up occurs among the residents ; officers' leave, except on particular cases, always ends at this time, the drilling season then coming on ; civilians gladly return to their full allowances, which, after a certain time spent in the hills, are partially withdrawn, and idle people willingly exchange what after a time becomes the dull monotony of the Himalayahs, for the more exciting and pleasant life of "the march." Some few individuals remain during the whole winter, but this is only where a constitution requires to be particularly braced up, and is not often resorted to. The population of the place diminishes in the course of October from 5,000 persons, or even more to one.

The Commander-in-chief, like the rest of the world, always takes his departure at this time, and commences a round of inspection of the different regiments and stations in the upper provinces, and accordingly in October our march began.

CHAPTER XII.

Bustle of Starting from Simlah - Mules *versus* Coolies—A Comfortless Night—Arrival in Camp—Native Chiefs—A State Dinner—Superiority of English Horses—Native Horsemanship Visit to a Native Prince—His excellent Character and Governmet—A Runaway Elephant—Caution on Snipe-Shooting—Visit to a chief—Incredulity of the Nativss about Steam—Visit to the Celebrated Colonel Skinner, a Half-casts Chief—Review of his Native Cavalry—Extraordinary Feats of Dexterit, on Horseback—Dinner of Ceremony.

October 25*th*, 1837.—To-day being the day fixed for our departure from Simlah, every one has for the two days previously been in a state of confusion and bustle. The noise (without which nothing can be done in this country) has been unceasing. What between squabbling among the Coolies, and fighting between masters and servants, Bedlam broke loose would be quietness in comparison.

Great difficulty at times occurs from the number of bearers required for baggage not being forthcoming, and at twelve o'clock I found myself without any ; and upon writing to the political agent and finding I was to get no redress, I sent to the bazar and succeeded in obtaining mules, which for the future I shall always use in preference to human cattle, as being both much cheaper and less troublesome.

We ourselves took our departure at three in the afternoo with many a longing look from some of the party at what we were leaving behind us ; but not from me, who, on the contrary, am very glad to be out of it, and to change the scene. We reached Cyrey, the first-stage bungalow, to tea ; and I passed the most uncomfortable night I have done in India, from sharing my bed with millions of fleas, who made a meal off my person the whole night ; and morning found my eyes still unclosed, and I made a mental resolve never again to sleep at Cyrey if it could be avoided.

October 26th.—We began our march at day-light, and a long and tedious one it proved, into Subattoo, where we took up our old quarters at a friend's house. Found, as usual in the beginning of a march, that some mistake had been made touching breakfast, and that not so much as a loaf of bread was forthcoming ; but Captain M., commanding here, made up for it by feeding us nobly at his house, he living quite *en prince*, as almost all the Indian officers do.

To my taste, the temperature of Subattoo at this season is preferable to that of Simlah, being 2000 feet lower and much warmer, but not so much so as to make one feel its effects disagreeably. In the evening we all dined with Captain M., whose excellent house and dinner made up for the previous night's discomforts. After a good hunt for any remains of my former nights's bedfellows, I turned in, and heard nothing till four in the morning of the 27th, when we commenced our last hill-march, and again passed through the country which we had all voted so terrile from precipices, but which *now* we look down upon with contempt, arrived once more in camp, with tired ponies as feverish brows, and found the heat awful in comparison to what we have for months been accustomed to. In spite of the warmth I, for one, am right glad again to find myself in my tent; and as my horses are all in good order, and every thing come up right, have nothing to diminish my pleasure. Our camp equipage meets us at the foot of the hills, having remained during the summer months at Kurnaul, the nearest station to the hills, one's horse being forthcoming from the same place; and most gladly do we exchange the dull movements and shambling pace of the mountain pony for the noble gallop of the Arabian.

October 28th.—A short march of eight miles through the valley of Pinjore to the gardens, meeting on the way two nobles of the Patialah court coming to congratulate Sir Henry on his arrival. They were well mounted, as most of that chieftain's people are, and their followers in very tolerable order. In the evening the gardens were illuminated as when we were in them six months ago, and we again had precisely the same allowance of nautching and fireworks as on the former occasion.

October 29th.—Left Pinjore for Monai-Majra, another eight-mile march. The Rajah of the latter place came out to meet us, with as ragged and dirty a suwarree as need be. He asked to be allowed to call on the General, which he is to do to-morrow. This worthy, being often drunk and always stupid and good-for-nothing, is only occasionally allowed the honour of visiting our great men, and the present treat was only permitted after much discussion.

With some little differences of opinion between me and my horses, who had not been mounted for the last six months, the remainder of the march passed off in peace. In the evening a large party of camp people dined here, which, as usual with such state parties, was anything but lively.

October 30.—A halt, to give time and opportunity for every one to arrange their equipage for the march, and get the escort and followers in order. The troops paraded in the morning for the chief's inspection, consisting, as usual, of half a regiment of infantry and one squadron of cavalry, furnished from Kurnaul. These troops are generally changed at the different stations, to prevent taking them too far from their own quarters.

The heat has to-day been unbearable, the thermometer up to 90°; and even at five o'clock, when we went out riding, it was by no means agreeable.

October 31st.—Marched to Bunoor, a small town in the dominions of the Patialah chief, and found the camp pitched on a wide, hot, sandy plain, covered with ruins and tombs of what seems to have been in its time a considerable place. In the afternoon Mr. C. lent me his English mare, and for the first time since I have been in the country I felt that no fence *need* stop me.

November 1st.—Our elephants had been ordered on to Sytabad, a very fine ruin of a large town of the Mussulman conquerors of India; at which place the Patialah Rajah had ordered his suwarree (or followers), to turn out to meet Sir Henry, He met us about a mile beyond the place, with a large and good-looking following. He himself seems a regular picture of the Pans of old, standing probably six feet five or six, with bone and strength in proportion, naturally; but the latter two qualities have been much diminished by his having had a continual illness for thirteen years. The whole road between Sytabad and the camp, pitched outside this chief's capital, was entirely lined with mounted matchlock men, in excellent order. in addition to a large body that followed his elephants; out of which last, one would occasionally spur his horse at full speed, trailing his spear behind him, and endeavouring to entice some other equally ambitions hero to attack him. When he succeeded in this object, some very showy and excellent horsemanship was displayed, and the picturesque and warlike-looking Seikh shewn off to great advantage. Altogether the show was an excellent specimen of a native court—scarcely inferior, I think, to Lahore—the people being generally better armed and clothed, though far inferior in numbers.

The Patialah Rajah has the largest territory, and rules it best of all the Seikh chiefs on this side of the Sutlej. He has the character of a good prince, father, and son; characters rarely to be met with among the higher princes and chiefs in India. The revenue he draws from his state, amounts to nearly thirty lacs of rupees (30,0000/.) regularly and well paid. He went with the General to his tents, passing round the walls of his capital, which seems in perfect order in every respect, and worthy of his name; and after having sat down for five minutes, Sir Henry named the afternoon as the time for our returning his visit, and departed.

At five the chief sent his son, a fat chubby looking boy of fourteen, magnificently dressed, to escort the General to his palace; which we reached, after passing through several of the particularly dirty and narrow streets of the town: his residence proved to be the best modern building we had seen in India. He received us in a very beautiful open colonnade, forming one side of a superb court-yard, covered over with carpets of crimson silk, and with its roof groined in a manner that would have done honour to the best workman in London. The outer walls and windows of the buildings which surrounded us were all uniform, and superbly carved in moresco work, chunamed (a composition made of shells, which bears a high polish) over, and shining like marble. The large revenue which the good government of this chief enables him to receive, and which is so much more than he spends, leaves him a considerable surplus for purposes of this kind, for improving his buildings, erecting bridges, &c. &c. His corps of Nautch girls is very good; and after staying half an hour to listen to their singing we started homewards, much pleased both with this chief, his country, and his people. He obtained a considerable addition to his territory and influence by assisting and doing every thing in his power for us during the late Nepaul war; for which good service, and his general good conduct, a considerable tract of country became his.

November 2nd—A halt, probably more acceptable to four-legged than two-legged animals. The Rajah came in the evening to pay his farewell visit, and afterwards we accompanied him to see the town illuminated,—if a thimblefull of ghee (melted butter) with a lighted wick in it can be called so: there were also some bad fire-works at his garden-house on the other side of the town. After being jolted to death by our elephants for six miles we came to the gardens, and remained on the top of a house for an hour, after which the adieus took place and we returned home. The town of Patialah was like every other Indian town, with the exception of being in some degree cleaner; almost all towns in the country being the same, varying only in this point. The streets are uniformly narrow, with lines of shops on either side, in which cross-legged sit a number of Hindoos, smoking the eternal water-pipe, and higgling for pice with their customers. Sweetmeat shops always abound; and the numbers of flies that congregate around and on them, as may be easily supposed, do not add to the delights of living in one of these places. On illuminations like the present, each shop is required to find a certain quantity of *ghee*, with a wick in it, and to place this in front of his shop; and when not looked too closely into these do not make a bad show.

On reaching camp we found two or three of the party sitting in the durbar tent in great excitement,—Miss F.'s elephants havin run away at the fireworks, and not having since been heard of. The lost sheep made their appearance, however, in ten minutes, having been in considerable danger from the beasts running under trees. The animals raced for several miles, clearing every thing in their progress, and defying the efforts of their mahouts (drivers) to stop them. The principal danger in these cases is from their running under trees, and thus crushing their riders ; for otherwise they have such perfect use of their legs that an accident from their falling rarely, if ever, occurs ; and no nullah's bank is too steep for them to crawl down one side and up the other. Instances are known in India of their swimming the Ganges, in the headlong course which fear occasions ; and, far from being stopped by this, to again continue their race on the opposite bank with unabated vigour.

November 3rd, 4th and *5th.*—Continued our course through very deep roads, good, for riding, but bad for bullock hackeries. The country is very tolerably wooded and beautifully cultivated. Some little snipe-shooting is, I believe, to be had in the neighbourhood, but the heat is too great for any one having a value for his liver to go out. Very many of the diseases in India which are laid to the change of climate, arise, I am convinced, by the continual exposure which this sport brings with it, which is both the best and commonest we have here. Young men on first coming out are immediately told, on asking about shooting, of there being excellent snipe in such a *gheil* (lake) close by. Fired at this, the youngster shoulders his gun ; finds, as he has been truly told, excellent sport ; remains out up to his neck in water, and with the sun upon his head at 150° the whole day ; and on the following is perhaps very much surprised to find himself with a fever, which he immediately lays down to this "infernal climate."

November 6th.—A short and pleasant march of ten miles to Sasaun, a dirty looking village, situated on a mound above very large tracts of rice-grounds, now as dry as the floor from the drought. There is an immense *gheil* (lake) in the neighbourhood, to which two of our party went in search for snipes this morning, with some success.

November 7th.—Marched into Kytul, the capital of a small principality ; whose Rajah has already drank up his drink, and become bedridden at the age of twenty-one. The political agent had fought hard to get Sir Henry off from paying him a visit, on the score of his health ; but he begged so hard, saying that his people would look down upon him if his prayer was not granted, that the agent was at last obliged to consent. Accordingly the General turned out of the road, followed by the cavalry of the escort, and paid him a short visit in his bed. He found him laid out in a large room of a very beautiful garden-house, which cost him a lac and 40,000 rupees (14,000*l*.) in building. I was sent back to call up the escort, and did not see him ; but those who did, and general report, described him as the most intelligent native they had seen.

We afterwards went through sundry dirty streets of the city to a gate close to the camp, to which the cousin and nearest relative of the chief accompanied us, armed with a particularly good double-barrelled Smith gun ; to get which he had travelled dak (palanquin travelling) to Calcutta, and returned by the steamer. He told us that on his telling his country-men the manner of coming up the river per steamer, no one would believe him ; and that even now, though not without a listener, he was without a believer.

November 8th.—Left Kytul for Balloo, where, through some mistake in the time by the Adjutant-general, we arrived before the sun was above the horizon.

November 11th.—Marched to Narnoon, where the camp is to halt one day previous to marching into Hausi.

November 12th.—Halt, and ride along the banks of the

canal, a beautiful running stream which (originally a work of the Mogul emperors) had been for some years filled up, but was again opened by our government about seven years ago.

November 13*th.*—Made our entry into Hausi, celebrated for a fortress originally built by George Thomas, and for being the station of Colonel Skinner's regiment of irregular horse. Skinner himself is a half-caste, and one of the darkest I ever saw, and was dressed half in the dress of the regular cavalry, and the remainder in that of his own corps, of which he had a squadron on the road to salute the General Their dress is, I think, more picturesque than handsome, being a long frock of yellow cloth, trimmed with black lambskin, or fur, and embroidered with the same material on the shoulders and breast ; a small casque, which fits close to the head, and high boots without spurs. The horse-appointments are entirely native, with the exception of a sheepskin over the saddle. Some of the native officer's equipments were very handsome, and their horses good ; but the men's were very plain, and their horses but very indifferent.

This station is now the most unhealthy in India. The newly raised corps (the Hurriona light infantry) have nearly 400 men in hospital, and twelve men already this month dead. This they ascribe entirely to the canal ; and the great object of the General's visit to the place was to see what could be done. With this object he rode round the lines in the afternoon, and from them certainly nothing could arise which would lead one to expect the place to be so fatal as it is. The Sepoys' lines were, I should say, better than those in nine-tenths of the stations, and far cleaner.

The canal just alluded to, which was re-opened and is kept up by our government, and to the irrigation from its waters around the station, is the nuisance which has of late been so deadly to be ascribed. Nevertheless, no people in the world, perhaps understand irrigation better than the natives of the great continent of India; and wherever water is to be obtained (no matter how far they have to bring it), the green and flourishing state of the country soon shews its natural riches, whenever this luxury can be come at. With the aid of water, the hot sun and rich soil soon produce a crop that would gladden the heart of an English farmer.

November 14th.—The General inspected Colonel Skinner's corps this morning. They looked remarkably well and showy, though of their efficiency I have my doubts. The corps turned out very weak in numbers, only 418 horses appearing on parade, the sickness taking away several, and large detachments, in every direction. They went through the regular cavalry movements remarkably steady and well, and if their horses *on service* can but do work, they would prove a efficient corps.

In the evening Colonel Skinner shewed the feats of horsemanship for which he and his corps have been so celebrated; it however proved, like most things in India, a failure. In shooting at the bottle from horseback, the bottle was only hit five times in two rounds by fifty men ; and bringing out the tent-peg on the top of a spear proved an entire failure.

Firing at the bottle is, in truth, a most difficult feat, and would puzzle many of our English riders and shots, particularly with that awkward weapon the matchlock. The way it is done is by a bottle being placed on the ground, parallel with which a horseman comes at full speed, passing it at some forty yards distant. When he has arrived in a straight line with the bottle he fires, his horse being at the time at full speed, and occasionally he hits it, Young Skinner, the Colonel's son, did so twice, and one or two of the native officers; but the men generally made a failure of it. The feat with the tent-peg is equally difficult. The peg is driven firmly into the ground, the horseman comes at it at full speed, and lifts it out of the ground on the point of his spear. This performance is even more rarely done than the other.

Much the best part of the spectacle was the men throwing themselves off their horses, and jumping on again, at full speed, in their heavy boots, and armed as usual, which several did with the greatest case. There are several corps of the same kind as this Skinner's dispersed over the country, formed originally on the one of same plan as his, and called "local horse;" though, with the exception of the present one, none of them are properly so, inasmuch as the others move from one station to another, in the same way as the regular cavalry. The men find their own arms, horses, and appointments, and receive a fixed monthly pay accordingly, but still under the same form of discipline as the rest of the Company's forces. With the natives it is generally a very popular service, and the men in this branch are commonly of a better stamp than those in the regular cavalry, where the habits of a native horseman are completely changed—where, in the place of a comfortably stuffed saddle, and a bit with which he can bring his horse upon his haunches with the slightest touch, we give him a heavy and uncomfortable cavalry saddle and the crooked bit of the English dragoons, neither of which equipments suits either his habits or his prejudices.

At night we dined with the old chieftain, Colonel Skinner, and had a most excellent dinner, having to meet us several ladies aud gentlemen, comprising the beauty and fashion of the station and neighbourhood. The evening passed most pleasantly; several of the party singing remarkably well; and in this out-of-the-way corner of the East, two voices might be heard very rarely equalled.

CHAPTER XIII.

Inspection of Native Infantry—Fast Travelling—Company's Breeding Establishment at Hissar—Use of Camels for Artillery—A Native Farm—Fort of Hausi—Farewell Dinner—Change of Route—A Native Prince—Sporting Party—The Imperial City of Delhi Its Present and Former State—Superb Street—Noble Mosque—Grand Dinner—Fine Sepoy Regiment—Magnificence of Ancient Delhi—Magnificent Column—Curious Iron Pillar—Extraordinary Feat of some Native—Royal Deputation—Fallen Greatness.

November 15th.—The General inspected the Hurriona light infantry, a corps raised last year by his order, in place of three regiments formerly stationed at the place, in the pay of the Begum Sumroo. Captain G, their commander, got very much, and deservedly praised, for the manner in which he had disciplined and got them in order; for no corps that I have seen in India, considering the disadvantages of sickness and recruiting under which they have laboured, can be at all compared to it, either in appearance or steadiness.

In the evening, with two brother aides-de-camp, I followed Sir Henry, who had gone on a-head in Colonel Skinner's carriage to Hissar, the station on the Company's stud, doing the fifteen miles, up to the Superintendent's house, within the hour—coming in in time for a second dinner. Every other part of the country that I have seen was a perfect garden, in comparison with the desert we passed through between the two places; nothing but continued plains of bare sand, with prickly shrubs sprinkled here and there, without even an attempt at cultivation. Captain Hailes, the superintendent, had most comfortable tents ready for us, and dinner enough to feed a regiment.

November 16th.—The day's work began with the inspection of the breeding part of the stud—the old stallions, mares, and young horses bred as stallions for the district. The mares (about 200), in and out of foal, were beautifully kept in loose boxes; and, as far as condition and health went, could not be in finer order. But these animals wanted weeding sadly, ont having either blood or bone enough to breed troopers from. The old stallions consisted of six through-bred English horses, and two Arabs, better, I think, in this stud, as far as these went, than any of the others. This portion of the establishment is supposed to be entirely for the breeding of young horses, to be sent into the district as stallions for the Zemindars, of which there were about thirty, which will be sent off in the course of a month. The system they go upon is to give out a certain number of mares and stallions into a tract of country, for whom the Zemindars, or cultivators, are responsible. These men are only too glad to get them, an excellent price being given for every yearling colt they bring in, and which they are not permitted to sell until the Company's officers have had first choice. Thus their interest is thoroughly engaged, and the system has been found to answer, both as to expense and in the number bred.

In the evening we rode through the enormous ruins of the ancient city of Hissar (which was a favourite summer residence of the emperors in the time of Feroze Shah) to the zemidary stables, or horses which have been brought up as colts of four months old, from the land-owners, and brought up from that time till they are as many years old, when they are draughted into the cavalry, if arrived at a proper height (14.2) and upwards. We saw about 750, of all ages, out of which 280, the whole of the four-years-old horses, will be brought before the committee in the course of a fortnight, and, if sound and large enough, will be drafted into the cavalry. The stables here, as well as the breeding stables, were, I think, superior to those either at Haupper or the central stud; but among the colts there were Former unexceptionable ones than in the two former, though the abuse which is lavished on the horses from it did not quite seem deserved. The price which these horses stand the Company in each, varies very much at the different studs, depending chiefly on the time the buildings have been finished, and the cost expended on them. This from being the last established, has hitherto been much the most expensive, each horse costing nearly 700 rupees (70*l*..) while those at the central stud are drafted into the cavalry at 400 (40*l*.) This price, however, has here been greatly diminished during the last two years, and the young horses now go from this stud at 400 (40*l*.), and at Gazipoor at 250 (25*l*.), every item included,—cost of stabling, horses, breeding, &c.

Attached to the stud are a superintendent, surgeon, and veterinary, together with several serjeants as assistants. Every horse is allowed three seer (6 lb.) of grain throughout the year, and ten pounds of grass. One seyce (groom) takes care of three horses, and the brood mares have one to every seven, who are paid four rupees each (8*s*.) per month. The establishment is by no means confined to horses, the Company keeping, in addition otall this, a very large breeding establisment, both of camels and bullocks. The gross returns give at this moment, 1532 hroses, 8283 camels, and 4117 horned cattle, under the charge of

Captain Hailes, the superintendent, according to the following official list, given us by him:—

Present state of the Company's establishment at Hissar, November 16, 1837.

Horses.			*Horned Cattle.*		
Stallions		117	Bulls		85
Mares		402	Cows		1576
Colts		875	Produce	Males	755
Fillies		138		Females	1044
Total		1532	Bullocks		637
			Total		4117

Camels.			*Total Animals.*	
Stallions		29	Horses	1532
Brood Camels		3566	Camels	8258
Produce	Males	2525	Cattle	4117
	Females	1671	Total	13907
Carriage		167		
Total		8258		

It was dark before half the stables had been gone through, and it was therefore arranged to see the remainder in the morning, and return home in the afternoon, after seeing the camel and cattle studs.

November 17th.—This morning we saw the remainder of the zemindary colts, and afterwards had several of the under-sized horses led out for the Quarter-master-general, who wanted two of them as carriage horses.

After the committee, which is composed of certain cavalry officers appointed for the purpose, have chosen those horses they think fit for the service of the dragoons, the remainder, that is, those below 14·2, are sold for the benefit of government, and make most useful little animals for carriage-horses, buggies, &c. &c. Of those that are chosen for the service, the horse-artillery have the first choice, the European dragoons the second, and the Indian light cavalry the third; which is a most fair arrangement, the horse-artillery and dragoons requiring far more powerful horses than their lighter neighbours, the Company's cavalry.

The bullocks bred here are of a very large size, for the use of the food-artillery and bublic carriages, and for almost every thing requiring draught in this country. The camels, in like manner, are chiefly for the use of moving troop stores, being at all times ready for emergencies, and are considered the finest bred in India.

In the evening, after seeing an enormous number of artillery and carriage-bullocks, we mounted our horses and galloped into Hausi in a little more than an hour.

November 18th.—The General looked at two pieces of artillery, which, being drawn by camels, excited some curiosity. As far as we could judge by their appearance on parade, they seem to answer admirably, dragging the gun through sand without the smallest difficulty. How far they will answer in wet weather remains yet to be proved.

Till of late that fine arm of the Company's forces, their artillery; was confined to two kinds,—one, the horse, drawn (of course) by horse ; and the other called the foot, intended to work with infantry, by bulloks. Major Pugh, an old and excellent artillery-officer, bethought him, some time ago, that camels might be well substituted for the latter, and drove both a faster and stronger animal for the service. Accordingly, he got Sir Henry to allow his fitting up a battery, each gun to be drawn by four camels, and the experiment has been found to answer admirably. The great objection raised against them was, that camels, from the form of their feet, could not work in wet water weather, in consequence of their slipping about ; but against this it was argued, that although this was the case with a camel with a heavy load on his back, it did not, therefore, follow that it would be the same with one with nothing but a light rider up him, and, moreover, partially supported by his harness. Camels are used for every purpose by the natives, except drawing, their hardiness, patience, and capability of carrying great weights, making them far preferable as beasts of burden to bullocks, which are more generally used on the Madras and Bombay sides of the continent. Since the experiment thus tried with guns, its projector had used them in drawing carts and wagons ; and, in short, had proved that it was only for want of a trial that they have not been found as useful on the hard road as on the sandy desert.

I rode afterwards, with General, to a farm of Colonel Skinner's, who shewed us some remarkably fine bullocks and buffaloes, and the only realy good bit of sugar-cane I have seen in the cauntry, some of that imported from Otaheite now beginning to be very much used in many parts of the continent.

The General inspected the fort of Hausi in the evening, which seemed a strong place, with mud ramparts and a very wide ditch. It was originally built by George Thomas, an adventure, originally a sailor, who was dispossessed in the time of the Mahrattas. Upon their fall it passed into our hands, since which time the works have been modernised and every thing put in complete repair.

November 19th.—The last day of our stay in Hausi was devoted to escorting some of our party to see Colonel Skinner's farm ; after which he gave a farewell dinner to all the military in the place, and on the 20th we left Hausi *en route* to Delhi. The want of rain having so dried up the country as to make it impossible for the General to continue his inspections towards Neemuch, our route is fixed to Delhi and Kurnal, beyond which nothing is known. The immense size of a camp like ours and the quantity of mouths to feed, make its irruption very serious affair in the country. The present season has been one of the most dreadful ever known in India, from the want of rain and the consequent failure of the crops ; and the cattle, corn, and other means of livelihood of the ryots and villagers having failed them' the addition of such a party as ours would bring starvation wherever we went ; and accordingly, our intended expedition to the westward, as far as the frontiers of the Bombay presidency, was of necessity given up, and we once more turned our heads towards Simlah, there to spend the winter as well as summer months. Though in some cases alleviated by a most liberal subscription, made throughout the country for the sufferers, and by liberal manner in which government gave work to a very large portion of the most destitute, still the starvaion was much too general for all cases to be taken in, and the scenes we witnessed every day will never be forgotten by any of us.

November 22nd.—Left Bura Bhowaine for Munheira, and on the 23d entered Dadree, where the General was met by the Nawab of Jhugger, who had come thus far (the extremity of his dominions) to met him. His riding-dress was by many degrees the best I have seen in this country. consisting of a thickly quilted coat of green *silk*, and boots reaching up to his knees of white doe skin, and silaer spurs. His people, oj whom he had not above a dozen with him, were all dressed alike in substantial, but plain appointments He himself is a very good-looking, gentlemanlike man, and bears the character of being an excellent master. The original holder of the Taghine principality was an Affghan, who commanded a body of horse under Lord Lake and at the time when the Company had more country than they know what to do with, he received this property; which has descended to the present owner, his grandson, with a revenue of nearly six lacs of rupees 600,000/.)

November 24th —Marched to Belontah, where some of the party went out shooting and had very decent sport, though every thing was very wild. They saw quantities of black partridge, hares, and hogs.

November 25th.—Marched into Jhugger, another of these petty chieftainships; the Nawab met the General a short distance from the town mounted and dressed as just described. He had two infantry regiments and some irregular horse drawn out for the chief to look at. The foot were dressed after the Comnany's Sepoys, and more decently than such native imitations generally are. His irregulars were particularly good, all dressed like himself, except that the articles were less costly; and they were, I think, rather better mounted than the usual run.

November 29th.—Last night we encamped within seven milcs of Delhi, and this morning entered the imperial city. For three miles before coming in sight of modern town, the road ran through ranges of ruined villas, temples, palaces, and serais, which yet shewed remains of what Delhi had been in the time of the emperors, and how fallen she now was from her high estate.

The Brigadier commanding here (General Fast), with General Ramsey, the general of division, came out two miles to meet the chief ; and in their comany we marched on to our camp, passing round the walls of modern Delhi (or Shah Jehanabad, as it is more properly called), which consist of the wall built by Shah Jehan and repaired and fortified by our engineers. We found the camp pitched in one long line opposite the Cashmere gate of the city, near a church built by Colonel Skinner within the walls.

In the evening I went with a party to see the great lion of the place, the Motee Musjid, one of the noble mosques. We entered the city by the Cashmere gate, and passing down by an excellent street, entered the Chandy Choke, the largest and best street in India, and which, I must own, far surpassed any thing I could conceive an Indian city to be. It is nearly a mile long and forty yards broad, leading direct from the palace to one of the gates of the town, and was, when we saw it, full of people and vehicles of all sorts, from the dog-cart to the four-in-hand. It is lined with shops on both sides, and seemed a very excellent bazar.

Passing through this street we went on to the Jumma Musjid (or place of Friday prayer), a superb building round a court-yard, with a small tank in the centre for the ablutions of true believers before and after prayers. It was built by Shah Jehan in the year 1632, and finished ten years afterwards. The whole exterior is of red sandstone, with the exception of the domes and minarets, which are of white marble. The whole place was full of people coming to evening prayers, or actually at them; so that, without taking off our shoes, they would not admit us into the interior, which however did not seem to be any thing remarkable. We went home by the Lahore gate, and finished the evening by a party at home.

December 1st.—Pestered the whole day by endless merchants and jewellers of all kinds. Some of the shawls and jewels were very beautiful, particularly the former, but much too expensive for a lieutenant of infantry. In the evening I rode through part of the town with General C. and looked through the palace gate, which seemed, as fas as one could judge by a momentary peep, to be worthy of the descendant of Shah Jehan. All the rest of the party dined at a grand dinner given to the General by the Brigadier, at which I was not obliged to be present.

December 2nd.—Review of all the troops in Delhi, consisting of the corps of Sappers and Miners, and the 38th, 48th and 16th regiments of Native Infantry, with two companies of artillery under Brigadier F., which proved much the same as all others of the same kind, proving, of course, a bore to all parties concerned.

December 3rd, Sunday.—Heard prayers and a sermon in a new and pretty church, built within the city walls by Colonel Skinner; I suppose, as some atonement for his misdemeanours while in the Mahratta service, which till then was an establishment much wanted by the Europeans of the place.

December 4th.—Inspection of the Delhi magazine, and in the evening that of the 16th and 38th regiments; the former, under Major Maclaren by far the finest regiment I have seen in the country, in particular, *averaged* upwards of six feet high; and throughout the regiment every thing,-clothing, setting up, and appearance in every way,—shewed what could be done with Sepoys by a little care on the part of the commanding officer. I have seldom heard the chief express himself more strongly than he did in praise of this regiment, to its commander. The great personal beauty, which I think exists more in this class of men in India than in any other I ever saw, was particularly shewn to-day, their tall and fine figures and moustached faces giving a very great example of it. The average height of the corps was also greater than that of any European regiment; and one cannot go down the ranks of one of our people without seeing the immense advantage the Sepoy has over him in personal appearance.

December 5th.—In the morning the General inspected the corps of Sappers and Miners under Captain Thompson. The men were nothing remarkable either in size or form, which in fact is not necessary for a corps of their nature. We walked afterwards through some of the works and mines, which to me, who do not understand that kind of thing, was by no means interesting. The chief saw in the evening the two remaining corps of infantry, both very fine regiments.

December 6th.—Started at day light to see the great lion of Delhi, the Cutub Minar, twelve miles from this on the Agra road. The ride to it was very interesting, shewing so well what must have been the size and magnificence of ancient Delhi. From the time of leaving modern Delhi, or Shah Jehanabad, as it is properly termed, the whole country was one continued mass of buildings, all more or less dilapidated.

We found our change-horses laid at a tomb which has in former times been very magnificent, but is now fast going to decay. It was erected to the memory of Suffter Jung, a favourite of one of the emperors. The gardens round it must in their time have been beautiful, but are now like the building they encircle, all gone to wrack and ruin. We aftewards went on to the Cutub, under which we found the tents pitched. This building has numbers of legends attached to it as to the cause of its erection; some say it was built for the favourite wife of its founder Cutub-ud-Deen, the founder of the line of the Patan sovereigns of Delhi, to view the goings on of the good people of Delhi. It is a superb piller, well worth coming to see, 242 feet high, and nineteen yards in cirumference at the base, covered with beautiful carying in stone of verses from the Koran. We went twice up to the top—a journey of no small expense, both in legs and expenditure of brain.

Among the other lions at the Cutub is a large iron pillar covered with characters, which the natives believe to go through the earth. Nadir Shah, during his invasion, fired a cannon at it, the mark of which still exists.

In the evening we amused ourselves by seeing four or five fellows jump in to a well ninety feet deep, which has a slanting passage for them to get out by from the bottom I believe, if the truth were known, this sight interested the majority of our party more than the Cutub. They did this with the greatest possible *nonchalance*, men and boys rushing, at the sight of a rupee, to see which could first throw themselves over The fellows make a regular trade of it, and no accident ever happens, so expert are they.

December 7th.—Came back from the Cutub, turnning out of the road to see the tomb of the Emperor Humaioon—a large handsome building, very much on the same model as the Taj, without the ornamental part of the inlaid marble, and afterwards we rode through the town into camp.

December 8th.—Lord C. and his lady joined our camp last night, intending to remain while we remain at Delhi, and then march to Kurnaul to see the cavalry brigade. In the evening the General received a deputation from the King of Delhi, in the person of his third son, a dirty, uninteresting-looking individual, who stared about him and seemed scarcely of understand what he was to do, having never before been outside the city walls in his life. The younger branches of the ancient royal family of Delhi are now in the last stage of ignorance, poverty, and misery. The British gvernment allow the fallen descendant of Timour 150,000*l*. a year, which the king is obliged to employ in feeding his numberless descendants, who are too numerous, to leave him in possession of enough to keep up even the little state he is allowed by us. Fallen, however, as they are, not the smallest iota of their dignity will they permit to be infringed upon ; and even the young scion was, after much fighting, allowed to enter the tent with his shoes on – a piece of impertinence which Runjeet sing, in all the grandeur, whould not have ventured to attempt. His suwarree and attendants were all in the dirtiest and worst possible taste—a bad attempt at show and magnificence ; while in reality the smallest rajah in the Seikh states would have cut a far better figure. He stayed about half an hour, during which it was arranged that Sir Henry's visit to the king should take place at eight to-morrow morning.

CHAPTER XIV.

Visit to the King of Delhi Fallen Greatness—A Royal Guard—"The Asylum of the Universe"—The Peacock Throne—Court Ceremonies—The present Monarches of Delhi—Extraordinary Jewels—The Kelat, or dress of Honour—Camel Artillery—Their extraordinary Speed—Departure from Delhi—City of Panipul—Scene of famous Battles—Magnificent Serais of Ancient Governments—Kurnaul—Indian Hospitalities—Reviews—Departure from Kurnaul—Encampment at Monai-Majra—Chattering Coolies—Arrival at Simlah—Gold in India—An Alarm—A Fire—A Snow-fall.

December 9th.—Made our visit of ceremony to the King of Delhi, which I had for many a day looked forward to with disgust, as I did not like the General so lowering himself as to stand in the presence of a dirty, miserable old dog like this man, after having been seated in the durbar of Runjeet Sing.

The Great Mogul still lives in the palace of his ancestors, if a ruinous mass of mud and dirt can be called such. We entered it by a very handsome gateway, which is kept by our Sepoys since some disturbance which took place three or four years ago, when the inhabitants shut the gates and refused to acknowledge the Resident's order for admittance. After passing through this gate, which shewed the remains of its former magnificence, we entered a large paved courtyard, surrounded by ruins, and filled with ragamuffins of every variety; through which we passed, and, turning to the left through an arched gateway entered several dirty streets lined with mud huts, and what the King calls his Sepoys—a band to which Hogarth's representation of the "March to Finchley" would be in comparison splendid. One fellow had a matchlock; a second an old rusty sword; another dirty rascal blew with all his might a trumpet, to which those of the archangel would have been penny whistles in comparison to the noise they made; a fourth fellow had bows and arrows. Every one was dressed and armed as suited his own fashion, and sundry and manifold were the habits thus displayed. Excepting the Rajah of Faroukabad's peopel's these outshone any thing we have before seen.

We arrived in time at a low archway, through which the General's elephant could not pass; so that they hoped he would be obliged to walk, which would give additional dignity to the king, as his people would suppose that the English chief walked so far to shew his respect for "the Asylum of the Universe." This charitable intention the General however balked, by getting into his jompawn, an open sedanchair; in which he was carried to the entrance of the courtyard, where was seated the King of kings.

This courtyard and hall of andience was about a hundred yards across, and on arriving in front of the red purdah (curtain) each of us was made to perform a low salaam. This being done, we crossed the court, and, entering by a side door, found ourselves in the colonnade room, which contained the angust presence of his majesty of Delhi, seated on the peacock throne. We were severally brought up and presented, each making a present of a certain number of gold mohurs (value sixteen rupees) according to his rank. The General, in the course of the day, gave 121; the major-generals, 11; colonels, 9; majors, 7; captains, 5.

The present king is a mean, vulgar-looking individual of sixty. He was handsomely dressed, and had on some really very fine jewels, particularly pearls. The throne, which is still called the peacock throne, was in the time of Akbar said to have jewels on it to the value of 20,000,000*l*. and Nadir Shah took from it upwards of 14,000,000*l*, A single diamond which formerly stood at the top, which is now replaced by a piece of glass (the Koh-e-noor), was valued at upwards of 3,000,000*l*.; and the peacocks which stand at each cornor han each a string of pearls in their beaks, valued at 100 000*l*. These, like the diamonds, are now replaced by false ones, and the jewels on the body of the throne have descended into coloured glass. The room, or open colonnade, in which this object stands, is very beautifully formed of white marble, inlaid with gold, and is still in tolerable repair, though the purdahs and carpets which compose its furniture in a sad state of dilapidation.

After each had been presented and paid his money, which his majesty took especial care not to lose, we were severally led away to receive the kelat, or robe of honour—a farce which the government still keep up, in spite of its marvellous absurdity. The General was robed in the king's presence, but we of the small fry marched into another room, to be made such figures as never were seen, even at Greenwich fair. Each of us had first a piece of rag tied round our cocked hats, by way of turban; after which a robe of spangled white muslin was thrust over epaulettes, sword, and all; over which again they treated each of us to a jacket of cloth of silver; and in this tomfool's dress we were again trotted across the court, obliged (which was the most difficult performance of the whole) to keep from laughing, and again to be presented to the king and be bedizened with a parcel of glass jewels and trumpery, to the value of two gold mohurs ; for which civility the company treated the king to another gold mohur from each.

While this was going on, three or four heralds were making as much noise as possible, by roaring at the top of their voices the titles and honours which had been conferred on the Commander-in-chief, and how much honoured he ought to be by the distinction conferred upon him by the "Asylum of the Universe." He was treated, to a coloured stick, which is, I believe, synonymous to to the baton of a field-marshal ; to the drums of state, which confer the power of life and death ; and to the following titels :—"The Line of the State"—"The Sword of the Empire"—"The Grandee of the Age"—"Sit H. Fane Bahadour, the strength of war."

This ceremony being concluded, we were again made to salaam, and, in the dress we had received, were trotted out to the gate to our elephants, and again went through the town ; I, for one, feeling more ashamed of myself than I had done for many a long year. We were not allowed to take off our dress till our arrival in camp, as that would have seemed disrepectful to his majesty ; and so strict is government on this point, that Mr. Fraser, the resident, some years ago, having thrown off his dress and given it to the beggars in the street, received a strong reprimand from his superiors, and was even threatened with the loss of his place.

Altogether, the ceremony is very ridiculous ; but still it is hard to deny to the fallen descendant of Timour the little deference and authority which is still left him.

The allowance or pension given by the Company to the old king would, were it not for his numerous relations and descendants, be sufficiently liberal, but these locusts consume all that can be obtained, thinking it beneath their high dignity, as princes of the land, to descend to earn their daily bread in that country where their fathers reigned as the most powerful and absolute monarchs of the earth. The consequence is, that the uncles, aunts, cousins, and relations to the most remote degree, live upon the sum allowed, namely, fifteen lacks of rupees, or 150/000*l*. per annum, and quickly reduce this sum to a very small portion, which the king can afford himself towards keeping up his own state. The late king of Delhi left behind, one of the most numerous families the world ever saw, and the present occupant of his throne promises fair, I believe, to equal his father in this particular. When our government first took him out of the hands of the Mahrattas a portion of territory immediately round Delhi was given him, which he was allowed to govern, and draw his revenue from, but after a very short time it fell off so much, from mismanagement, that the Company took it under their own superintendence, giving him a fixed revenue instead.

We went in the evening to see the newlytried camel artillery go eighteen miles an hour along the road, which they were supposed to be able to do. Whether they *quite* did it or not I will not say, but the pace they went at was quite sufficient to keep our horses in a gallop.

Decembe 11th.—Church, and farewell ride round cantonments, the first day, and on the second, left Delhi *en route* to Kurnual, and encamped twelve miles from the city, at Alleepore, a place in no way remarkable, unless it be for dust.

December 15th.—Marched to Paniput, a considerable city even now, and famous for having been the scene of more than one battle on which the of India depended. The principal one was that between the Emperor Baber and Ibrahim II. of Delhi, which ended in the defeat and death of the latter, and the capture of Delhi by the conqueror ; and again, between Shah Abdalla and the Mahrattas, in which the emperor slew some 30,000 of the invaders.

We rode through the town in the evening, which possessed no particular attractions, except being better paved and in more order than is usual. There is also a tomb of great sanctity which we also saw, and which proved very much like hundreds of others that we have seen. Paniput has, in times past, been defended by a fort and rampart, and could at any time be made defensible from the high ground on which stand the ruins of the former.

December 16*th.*—Left Paniput for Garonudah, where we halt to-morrow, previous to enternig Kurnaul. Near the camp is a handsome serai, with a gate built by Khan Feroze in the time of Shah Jehan. These serias, as they are called, or in a more known name, caravanserais, formerly existed at stated distances on the great road between Delhi and Lahore, for the accommodation of travellers, and were noble monuments of the great Moguls. But now all of them are going to wrack and ruin, and what few remain in tolerable repair have been converted into villages, and are filled with mud huts and the dirty varieties of an Indian village. All the successive governments that have ruled in India for centuries have left some public benefits in the shape of buildings, or other things, to mark their rule, save our own ; and if we were turned out of the country to-morrow nothing would remain, after a short time to shew that such a government ever existed. Keeping a few of such edifices in order would have greatly benefited our own people, and left some creditable marks of our presence ; but this is now too late.

December 18*th.*—Entered Kurnual. the General met, as usual, by all the station staff, &c. No end of hospitable invitations while we remain in the country. Dined this evening with a large party, to which were bidden all the great people of the place, and, as usual in India, the table actually groaned under the weight of sheep and oxen, by portions of which it was covered. Among other things, I observed three legs of mutton between me and my opposite neighbour, in size and excellence quite equal to that reared in our own country.

December 19*th.*—The General inspected the Queen's 13th Light Infantry, a very fine corps, part of which we had at Lahore last year. We had a view of the hills for the first time, at parade. The regiment performed remarkably well, and Colonel S. received much praise, which he really deserved. With the exception of the 31st, is is the finest corps I have seen in India. We dined with them in the evening at a very good and well-arranged dinner, sitting down some sixty to a table.

December 21*st.*—The artillery shewed off in the afternoon with round and grape shot, and afterwards sprung a mine, at which I was unable to appear from illness. The same cause prevented my having the *pleasure* of dining with the station in the evening.

December 22*d.*—The last day of our stay here, which began with a review of the Queen's 13th Light Infantry and the 27th N. I. the 3d and 4th regiments of cavalry, with a troop of horse-artillery, all under General D. ; and on the following day we marched out of Kurnaul to Leelakerie, the first march on the Loudhiana road, which we all remember well as the scene of a miserably rainy and disagreeabe day last year; on our way to Lahore.

December 24*th,*—Pitched near Thunesur, a place which was in former times, very extensive, but has, of late years, entirely gone to ruins. It is now, however, again fast rising into importance under Mr. C.'s judicious superintendence, and will probably, in a few years, become again a place of trade.

December 25th to 31st—Nothing worthy of recording, except that yesterday (the 30th) we reached that foot of the hills and encamped at Monai Majra, on precisely the same spot we occupied last year; and to-day I got a tumble from my pony, while jumping a bank and ditch, which has (I fear) put an end to my repeating that experiment for many a day.

January 1st, 18 8,—A miserable new-year's day, being spent in marching in a palanquin, on my back, all day, with fifty leeches on my side, which has just happened at the most disagreeable time. to-day, the 2d, as we left Pinjore for Burr, and again took up our old quarters under the hill, surrounded with Coolies, to whose talking Bedlam would be quiet in comparison.

January 3rd.—Made our first march through the hills to the Fur bungalow ; experience this time teaching us how much better this is than going up the long Subatto hill, for the mere pleasure of coming down again ; and on the 4th arrived safely at Hurripore, and found it also a far better bungalow than any beyond Simlah.

January 4th.—Took up our quarters, during the day, at the old and dirty bungalow at Sirai, which, if possible, looked more miserable than ever, and made our party glad to get out of it. and start at two for Simlah, where we again took up our old quarters about five o'clock. My abode is however. changed, and I now live in the General's own house ; which, in this weather, is decidedly a change for the better.

January 6th.—Out walking this morning we broke off a piece of ice from the tank, measuring three inches and a quarter in diameter ; which proves the cold to be greater in reality than even it is to our feelings, though I think to them it is quite as much so as is agreeable.

We have all been terribly alarmed at a fire that broke out in the chimney of one of the rooms, which, for some time bid fair to burn the house down. It was luckily found out by one of our party hearing a brick fall in the verandah of her room, which on her lifting up proved to be red hot, and on examination the whole of the beams in the roof were found to be on fire. By great good luck the Coolies had not been paid off, and by their help in bringing water we succeeded in getting it under, after the house had been almost given up as lost. Masses of ice were placed on the hot wall, and on melting answered the best of purposes. We did not however, succeed in extinguishing the fire until one wall of the house was in part pulled down. The Simlah houses are in most instances flat roofed, wet mud being placed upon them, and by successive thumpings finally wrought into a hard cake, making an excellent roof.

Some of the ice brought up for want of water was more than eight inches thick, which, if told in England, people would scarcely believe.

February 4th.—The first day's snow, which began in the afternoon, and lasted some two hours; sufficient, however, to cover the ground two inches thick, and to give a most cheerful wintry look to the place. Many of the staff, who had not seen snow-balls. Even to us, to whom it is not quite so new, it is an almost equal pleasure, as we have not now seen either snow or rain since Jully; and if it is only for the poor devils of peasants, it is enough to make one most happy.

February 10th and 11th—Heavy storms of wind and rain, and much snow on all the neighbouring hills, though Simlah itself has not been treated to any. Both the ground and trees on Mahassoo are perfectly white, as are all the hills on that range.

We remained quietly shut up for the two following months, thoroughly enjoying the bracing air and deliciously cold climate of the hills. We had for Simlah but little snow, and, excepting from frost, which made the roads too slippery for riding, nothing came in our way to prevent our duly appreciating the luxury of having such a place to spend the winter in. With the exception of our own people, and some few persons up here for their health, the society was much reduced from its usual size, and the roads looked comparatively deserted, which continued till the commencement of the hot weather, when it was again as full as ever.

CHAPTER XV.

Excursion up one of the Himalayah Mountains—A Mountain Prince—Intense Heat in the Mountains—A Narrow Escape—Unrivalled Scenery—A mountain Village—Dangers and Difficulties of the Ascent—Immense Size of the Trees—Summit of the Mountain—A Disappointment—Descent of the Mountain—Attack of a Leopard—Arrival at Simlah—Extraordinary Heat—A Three Months' Shower.

At certain seasons of the year continual parties are made to the Chour mountain, the snowy range, and, in a smaller way, picnics to Mahassoo, the next range of mountains to that of Simlah, towards the snowy mountains. The time for these expeditions are either immediately before, or immediately after, the rains: before, because the snow has been melted by the summer sun; and after, because it has not yet began to fall again, and thus to block up the pass through the mountains. The time at which we started on one of these excursions was too near that of the rains to permit our going all the way to the snowy range; and the additional reason of escorting a lady part of the way from Simlah to the rival hill station of Landour, formed a sufficient excuse for preferring the Chour, a mountain seventy miles from Simlah, and the highest of all the lower ranges of the Himalayahs in the neighbourhood.

June 2d.—We left Simlah in company with Miss F., Captain and Mrs. P., and Miss B.; and arrived at the first bungalow at Fargoo without an adventure, two of us riding the whole march, the remainder being in their jompawns ; and found tents and every thing most comfortably prepared expedition.

June 3d—Left Fargoo *en route* for Scinge, a small village about 5000 feet below, and the residence of a petty Rana, or mountian chief, who has a revenue of some 1500 rupees (150*l*.) annually. My companion and myself mistook our road, and wandered at least two miles in the wrong direction, before the people sent after us were able to to come up, Right glad we were to find ourselaves at our new ground, the heat being nearly that of the plains.

Our evening's amusements were much enhanced by the visit of a fat lout of a boy, calling himself Rana of place, who brought some wild raspberries as a present, and who very quietly waited before us and took the rupee we paid him for them, without the smallest idea that his dignity as a mountain prince was at all diminished by such a proceeding. His house stood a few hundred yards from our little encampment; a large uncomfortable-looking residence, something in the style of Swiss one, only far more dirty, the lower part being set apart for the cattle, sheep, and goats of the family, while the human part of the establishment occupied the higher story.

June 4th.—Remained during the whole day roasting at Scinge, the thermometer never standing at less than 96° in the tents; and at dinner time, at two o'clock, it was up as high as 90°. Even in the plains I do not think I ever felt greater heat. It was, however, so for an agreeable place, that I got a most delightful bathe in the river below the Rana's house, of which the drawing is but an indifferent sketch. The water was just the proper depth, and not too cold.

We left this furnace at half-past four, and commenced the the worst ascent in the hills. The first mile was a nearly perpendicular rise from the stream, with a very bad and narrow road; after which, the road ran along the side of the mountain to another stream, where my companion and myself dismounted, and taking off our caps, put our mouths to the water, and got rid of the thirst which the heat of the old encampment had caused. We now ascended, direct from the stream, up a nearly perpendicular hill to an elevation of nearly 7000 feet.

We met but with one adventure in our way, which happily went off without any serious misfortune. Miss B.'s pony slipped his hind legs over one of the precipices by the side of the road, and went down some twenty feet, when her presence of mind luckily got his head round, and stopped him. We arrived at our fresh ground late in the evening, after what seemed to be the longest march that I had ever made in the hills, though it was not really so.

June 5th.—Remained during the day comfortably under the trees at a beautiful village called Diah, and in the evening again commenced the ascent towards Putternullah, through a very beautiful wood of cedar and holly, which enlivened the first part of the road; and in the latter, the scenery was much too beautiful and grand to require aven the assistance of trees. I have seen nothing to be named in the same day with the latter part of this march, during the whole time I have been in the Himalayah. The hills were very much more grand and perpendicular in appearance than anything in the lower ranges. We found our camp pitched under a high cliff which crowns the Putternullah range, surrounded with ceder and other beautiful trees; and, in spite of predictions from a party when we encountered coming from the Chour yesterday, we met with no maladventure during the night from leopards or any other wild animals.

June 6th.—Left Putternullah at our usual marching hour of half-past four. For the first few yards we ascended perhaps as much as 500 feet, after which the road ran along a ridge of steep and precipitous crags, beautifully covered with woods of yew, mountain-ash, and sycamore. About half-way between Putternullah and Kugna, the road to Mussoorie branches off to the front, while that towards the Chour begins to descend, and continues to do so, passing over several mountain streams, and by two considerable villages. The tents were pitched on the opposite side of a large mountain stream near the village of Kugna. Had our usual game at cards, and turned in to pass the most uncomfortable night I have ever spent in India, what between the flies and the heat; not to mention that one's tent being place on the side of a mountain, the place of which one's bed stood was some eight inches higher at the head than the foot.

June 7th—Left Kugna for Serai, the last march before ascending the Chour. The road was for too narrow to be pleasant, in many places not more than two feet and a half, and sometimes even less, in width. Some parts of it were pretty, but, generally speaking, it was not at all so. The latter part was up one of the many streams springing from the Chour mountain, which brought us to the village of Serai (a large one of some thirty good-sized houses) and to the encamping ground, just at the foot of the commencement of the ascent, where all necessary supplies are to be had at the village where there is a jemadar (steward) belonging to the Rana of Joubul. Our own people having had a long march the day before, we determined to have what people we required to ascend the mountain fresh from the village, and accordingly ordered enough to take up one tent and things for tiffin.

June 8th.—Turned out of bed at half-past four, and after a light breakfast began the ascent of the Chour. One of our party and myself started on our ponies with the determination to rideas far as possible, but both soon gave up the attempt in despair : I, after the first quarter of a mile; and the other, after the first half-hour. The ladies of our party ascended in jompawns (the mountain chairs), with a double number of people to carry them; who were most necessary, having in many instances to lift the entire article over huge blocks of rock and fallen trees, and always to have an additional relay to pull in advance, the nearly perpendicular sides of the mountain requiring a lift from the front.

The road, or rather footpath, for it was nothing else, was as nearly perpendicular as it is possibe to conceive—mere steps in the rock, with enormous trees across the path in every direction. I did not think such a place existed in the world. All the moun- I have hitherto seen were mere molehills in comparison with this; for between four and five miles it was literally like a staircase, only not nearly such good walking, from the dead vegetation of the pines. It was the most severe walk I ever took in may life, and by the time I arrived at the top I was almost beat. The whole distance was through a forest of the leargest trees I ever saw, and in coming down we measured one of the largest, which was twenty-two feet in circumference ; and there were many which measured twenty.

After ascending in this manner about three miles and half, you come on a narrow plain running along a ridge, covered with huge blocks of granite, some of them hundreds and thousands of tons in weight. Passing along this plain, and over some of the granite blocks, we arrived at the tents, pitched under an enormous block close to a small temple and a well of beautiful water, the latter most grateful after such a march. I found myself at the tents half an hour before the others, their people taking so much time to get their vehicles up the mountain.

After resting for an hour, we again commenced ascending the remaining 500 feet, where even the ladies were obliged to walk. This part was nothing but immense massess of granite, covered in many places by decayed vegetation, from which the snow had just melted off. Many flowers, unknown below, were on this elevated spot (12.400 feet above the sea), the most beautiful of which was the wild onion, with a delicate white flower.

The extreme summit of the mountain was a large heap of stones, with a wooden post in the centre, on which the names of aspiring and perspiring individuals were carved, and to which I added those of our party. Unluckily, it was not a clear day; and the view, the chief object of our coming, was lost. On fine days, the Sutlej Jumana, and Ganges, are to be seen from this, as are the two hill-stations of Mussoorise and Simlah; but to day all this was invisible, and our labour is vain. I was however, well rewarded; and would not have missed the expedition for much. The ascent took the ladies in their jompawns four hours to accomplish, exclusive of the last 500 feet. It took me, walking, three hours and a half, and in the descent they were two hours and ten minute, and we much the same. I thought the latter worse than the former, the road being so slippery that I fell at least half-a-dozen times. We arrived in camp again at half past five, with appetites well wound up for dinner.

June 9th.—Heavy storms of wind and rain, sufficiently so to wet the tents and make extra Coolies necessary. When tents once become thoroughly so, it takes very many hours, and in damp weather even days to dry them, and when this is once the case their weight becames extreme, and what one coolie, or bearer, formerly carried, two will scarcely accomplish. Coolies never being the most hard-working class of the community, think themlseves very hardly treated, at having to carry any extra load of nay kind, and it is not a very uncommon occurrence for a party to take to their heels and leave you and your baggage to fate. The rain held up in the evening, and made our march the more agreeable. It was rendered less so, however, by the thought that it was the last we were to have together, part of our party going from the next halting-place direct to Landour. We made the march without adventure, and arrived at some new ground nearer the village than that we encamped on before. The noise made by the Coolies going with the Mussoorie parties' advanced tents, prevented all chance of sleeping till two o'clock, independently of having to get up once or twice to apply a stick their backs to prevent their making more noise than was absolutely necessary.

June 10th.—Part of our party left us this morning, much, I acknowledge, to our sorrow; and started at six o'clock on their way to Mussoorie, leaving us to comfort ourselves with slight showers and occasional heavy squalls of wind. Marched, as usual in the evening, through the old woods of holly and yew to some new ground near Putteraullah, far preferable to the old in the hollow.

June 11th.—During the night, one of our three goats was seized on by a leopard, and carried off down the cudd (valley). About half-past twelve I heard a faint struggle and groan, and then a howl from the servants, which was all they did in attempting to save the poor devil. They brought me the remains of the goat this morning, half-eaten up; and none of the party would have troubled themselves to get this, had not the Coolies wished to make a feast of the remainder. These animals (the leopards) were formerly far more common in the Himalayah than at present; when English sportsmen did not exist to kill them, and English ladies to by their skin: and in those times many were killed in the immediate neighbourhood of the present station of Simlah, but now one is rarely seen near it.

The wind blew cold and strongly over the elevated ridge

(nearly 10,000 feet) on which our tents were pitched, thohgh the thermometer stood at 60°, and we commenced the descent to Diah at half-past four, and found our canvass homes pitched on a beautiful piece of plain ground, about half a mile beyond the village, where I should recommend every one coming this road to place themselves, being very far preferable to that at the village, where flies and dirt are too plentiful to allow of agreeable encamping-ground.

In the evening we marched to Scinge, of roasting memory; but this time, become wiser by experience, we merely halted for the night and started up the hill again at daylight. Had another delightful bathe in the Giree, and concluded the evening much as usual. Were it not for the extreme and dangerous heat of these mountain valleys, excellent trout fishing might be had in almost all the many streams which take their rise in the snowy range, more especially in the one we crossed this morning; but the man is a rash one who ventures to risk his health by standing long beside them, the mountains rising so perpendicular on either side that the breeze cannot reach one, and the heat is thus rendered almost insupportable.

June 13*th.*—A most comfortable and long march back to Fargoo, where we again found ourselves about nine in the morning. In the evening though at the hot season of the year, our room was so cold that a fire was voted most agreeable, in spite of the smoke, for which this government-house is famous.

June 14*th.* Once more arrived at Simlah, after a trip in which we have been most fortunate both in companions and weather, and found the heat far greater than has been known in Simlah for many years. The thermometer in the house standing 86°, and rising out of it to 150°.

June 18*th.*—The rains set in this morning with heavy storms of wind and thunder, which in the course of a couple of hours lowered the thermometer 12°, and made the thermometer bearable.

* * * *

The rains, after continuing three months almost without ceasing, held up at last about the 12th of september, and the weather has once more become beautiful.

The first setting in of this periodical waterspout is at times quite superb. The heat generally has been very great, and a perfectly cloudless sky in every direction sorrounds you, when suddenly the heavens are overcast, claps of thunder resound among the hills in every direction, with lightning in great quantities: first the plains become hid from view; gradually range after range of mountains follows the same fate, till at length the water pours down as if a sluice had of a sudden been loosed; and for the next three months nothing is thought of but the best method of stopping the leaks in your housetop, and how one is to manage a short walk between the showers. During this season of the year, gaiety of all kinds is at a stand-still; few ladies choosing to risk their health and white satin shoes in a jompawn; and most people are content with the society of their own families, and of of the clouds which are at all times walking through one's house.

Nothing can be more perfect than the Simlah climate after the rains, till the time people usually go down to join their regiments or staff situations. At no time in England can we boast of such; the cold being just sufficient to make a fire desirable without being too much so for pleasure.

CHAPTER XVI.

Objects of the Expedition to Herat—Historical Sketch of the Affghan Princes—Leave Simlah—Parting Regrets—Camp Amusement—Leave-taking—Horse Disease peculiar to India—Sir W. Cotton joins the Camp—Projected Meeting between the Governor-general and Runjeet Singh—The Sutlej—Arrival of Lord Auckland—Meeting between Lord Auckland and Runjeet Sing—Awful Crush of Elephants—Extraordinary Scene at the Durbar.

Our expectations of seeing England in the course of the next twelve months have come to nothing, from an event happening, as agreeable as it was unexpected namely, the forming of an army on the north-west frontier, and Sir Henry taking the command of it in person. The causes which led to the formation of this army were these;—The Persians having been for some time besieging Herat, the capital of the small portion of territory which yet remains to the royal family of Affghanistan, and being under the influence of Russia, who would by its fall gain an accession of influence not approved of by the government, the Governor-general has determined, if possible, to raise the siege; and the force ordered to assemble, the General was offered the command of in person. This force is to consist of twelves regiments of native troops, three of European, three regiments of dragoons, two of irregular horse, and a large force of artillery; the whole to assemble on the Sutlej, to march thence along its banks to the Indus, and aftrr its arrival at Skikapoor, near which it was expected to join that of Bombay, to take advantage of circumstances. Herat having, by the gallantry of its defenders, assisted by Lieutenant Pottinger, managed to beat off its assailants, the army destined for Heart advanced upon Affghanistan,—the history of wkich I have here given a short sketch which will explain how matters stood at this time.

Ahmed Shah, an Affghan, and one of the principal generals of Nadir Shah, the liberator and usurper of the Persian monarchy, after the murder of his master withdrew with the Affghans in his service from the Persian army, and succeeded with them, assisted by some treasure he had obtained which had come to Candahar for Nadir, in making himself master of his native land, and was proclaimed King of the Affghans, with the title of Dooree Dooranee (the pearl of the age).

Ahmed Shah reigned twenty-six years; during which he four times invaded India, and twice marched as conqueror to Delhi; but the constant fatigue of body and mind which he endured brought his carrer to a close in June 1773, leaving his crown to his son, Timour Shah.

The Government remained in this weak prince's hands for twenty years, and dying he left behind him an immence family, of whom three only have any thing to do with our present relations with the country; namely, Shah Suja and Shah Zemann by one wife, and Mahmood by another.

At his father's death, in 1793, Shah Zemann proclaimed himself king at Caboul, and sent an army under his vizier against his elder brother Humaioon, who had seized Candahar. The latter was defeated and blinded, while Zemann's authority was allowed over the entire empire, his brother Mahmood being permitted to remain in command at Herat.

The Shah might now have reigned in peace had it not been for his worthless vizier, whose authority he insisted upon upholding; and, in doing so, put to death six of the most powerful nobles in the country who had rebelled against it. This having bred great discontent, his brother Mahmood seized the opportunity for revolt, having previously made three attempts for the crown in 1794, 97, and 99; and being this time assisted by Futteh Khan, the ambitious chief of the powerful Baurickrye tribe, succeeded in making himself master of Candahar.

Zemann, who was near the Indus preparing to invade India, immediately returnd to Cabul, leaving his brother Suja with the principles crown jewels at Peshawer. After much hesitation he did at length march against Candahar with an army of 30,000 men; but, on nearing the army of Futteh Khan, the van of the royal army went over to a man; which so alarmed the Shah and his vizier that they fled back to Cabul, where meeting with but little sympathy they again fled to the Shaurwaree country, and soon afterwards delivered Shah Zemann into the hand of Mahmood, by whom he (Zemann) was blinded, and his vizier put to death.

The new king gave himself up to enjoyment, and the dissensions among the nobles leaving the people at the mercy of the soldiery, an insurrection was raised, and Mahmood deposed, after having reigned two years, Shah Suja coming to the throne in his stead. Mahmood's eyes were spared and Zemann restored to liberty; the first an act of clemency, which Suja had afterwards reasons to repent of.

Continual rebellions and disturbances, some started by the new vizier, some by Futteh Khan the old, occurred in the country in one of which Mahmood, the late king, escaped and fled to

Furrah near Herat; and though the Shah was on the whole successful, still the country was far from settled when Mr. Elphinstone arrived at the court, in January 1809, on a mission from our government. Soon after this, while the vizier and his best army were employed in reducing Cashmere, Futteh Khan, the late vizier advanced upon and took Candahar; and this news had scarcely arrived when the terrible intelligence of the total defeat of his Cashmerian army arrived also.

In spite, however, of these disadvantages, the Shah raised an army and advanced upon Cabul, which his brother Mahmood had taken possession of, on the 17th of April, 1809. Mahmood's army under the vizier, Futteh Khan, met that of Suja between Peshawar and Cabul; when the latter was totally routed, and the unfortunate Shah fled to Peshawar and afterwards to Candahar, where a transient gleam of sunshine again shown upon his cause— an insurrection, at the head of which was the brother of his late vizier and other lords, having arisen in his favour.

Again a battle was fought near Chandahar, and again the fortune of Futteh Khan, Mahmood's vitzier, carried every thing before him ; and the unfortunate Shad finally crossed the Indus at Bukker and joined his family at Rawul Pindee, in the northern part of the punjab.

He was received by Runjeet Sing with many professions of respect ; and being prevailed upon again to try his fortune by the rebel governor of Kashmere, he crossed the Indus, attacked and took Peshawer, but was again obliged to cross that river in September 1810 ; and a similar attempt in the following year was equally unsuccessful : and being invited to visit Cashmere shortly after this by the governor of the province, he was seized and imprisoned by him : his family hearing of this fresh mistortune, seeking refuge with the Seikh monarch at Lahore.

Shah Suja being now disposed of, Mahmood succeeded in

fixing himself at Cabul, where, with the assistance of his vizier, Futteh Khan, he managed to defeat all attempts against his power, neither few nor far between till his cruelty to that extraordinary man finally lost him his crown. An insult he had committed in violating the sanctity of part of the royal haram some time before, and the royal family's fear of the vizier's growing power, finally produced his downfal ; and shortly after having defeated the Persians before Herat, on his refusal to give up the town to Kamrawn (Mahmood's son), he was blinded with the greatest cruelty, and sometime afterwards put to death.

This impolitic measure drove all the many and powerful brothers of the vizier into rebellion ; and, after many changes of fortune, the tyrant and his son were obliged to fly to Herat ; while Dost Mahommed Khan, one of the brothers, took possession of Cabul, two more of Candahar, while a third was made governor of Cashmere, and others appointed to the government of Jelalabad and Peshawer.

Thus was lost to the descendants of Ahmed Shah Dooranee that fine monarchy which he had left behind him, the rival brothers being one exiled to Hindoostan, the other to Herat.

In the meantime Shah Suja, released from his imprisonment, took refuge with Runjeet Singh who, however treated him in a manner unworthy of his great character, keeping him for several days without food, and finally obliging him to give up all his mest valuacle jewels. Runjeet rapacity did not end here, and the royal family, finding they were not likely to be allowed to remain in peace, effected their escape to our territories, where they arrived in December 1814, and were kindly received and pensioned by the governor-general.

After their departure the Shah was more closely watched, but nevertheless succeeded in escaping from Lahore, and marched to Kishtewaur, the Rajah of which tried to assist him in recovering Cashmere : in which however, as usual, he was unsuccessful ; and, after many wanderings, he at last was able to rejion his family at Loudiana, where, up to the present time he has lived a pensioner of our government till the aspect of affairs in Affghanistan determined our government once more to replace him on his throne.

The worthy Shah might, however, have remained unheard of and unseen, had it not been by the diminution of our influence in central Asia, and the rise of that of Russia ; the consequent attack of the Persians upon Herat, influenced by that power ; and the preference shewn by Dost Mahommed Khan, the ruler of Caboul, for the advice of the Russian agent, over that of Sir A. Burnes, the English political agent.

Dost Mahommed had long been at war with the Seikhs, had lost some of the finest part of his territory, and naturally wished for the alliance of a European power, from whom he might obtain both money and assistance. Our agent was not allowed to offer him either one or the other, but to give him plenty of advice ; while the Russian gave him no advice, but plenty of promises of supply, both of men and money ; and, it is believed, a little "ready" to back it.

Under these circumstances, it is but natural that this prince should prefer the Muscovite to the English alilace ; but this, nevertheless, formed the accusation against him and proved the means of dethroning and sending him from the country he had ruled with honour to himself and advantage to his subject.

Accordingly, some three months before the present time, certain officers were appointed to raise 7000 men for the service of the Shah, to be drilled and armed according to the Sepoy principle, and officered by Europeans.

Time did not allow the selection to be very good; and, from what I have lately seen, I fear it will be many a day before these troops will be of much use either to their master of any one else. With a sufficiency of time almost any nnmber of men can be raised for our service in India, the pay being excellent; the duty, except in cases like the present, not over great; and, above all, a pension, amply sufficient for all the moderate desires of the sepoy in his old age. Many causes, however, made it in the present instance not an easy matter:—firstly, as I said before, only a couple of months being given to raise so large a body in; secondaly, the knowledge that they were destined to fight against a race celebrated throughout the East for their bravery and fanaticism; and thirdly, and above all, their being immediately marched into a country where the sun had comparatively little power, and the snow was known to lie some four months in the year, interfering sadly with the comforts of a set of men whose religion makes it necessary for them to be almost naked while cooking and eating their food, and who ought, if orthodox Hindoos, to bathe after every meal.

November 3rd.—For the third time leave Simlah to commence marching, though looking forwards to very different end—to that of again returning to the old house and the old station stupidity. I must say that much as I have disliked Simlah, I now leave it with regret, having got accustomed to its monotony, and more particularly to one's house and establishment there. I quitted it with a heavey heart, and walked to the foot of the Gaute, mounted, and arrived with the General at Sirea, where we breakfasted remained during the heat of the day, and in the afternoon proceeded to Hurripore; thus avoiding the bugs and other *agremens* of the first bungalow.

November 4th.—Left Hurripore for the Furtices bungalow, where we arrived without adventure in three hours, and on the

5th, his Excellency having chosen to remain in bed instead of proceeding, as usual, on his March, desired the rest of his party to proceed, saying that he would join us in the evening at Bahr. This we accordingly did and arrived after a pleasant, though latterly a somewhat hot march, once more in camp, and again took up our old quarters in the midst of camels, elephants, Coolies, and noise

November 6th.—Left Bahr for Pinjore, where we found our camp pitched as usual. In the evening we had a bad Nautch and entertainment, the Patialah making it a rule to give us one every time we pass this, but without much variety.

November 7th.—Marched to Monai-Majra for the fifth time in my life, and probably the last. In the evening had a canter round some of my old haunts, and concluded the evening (the last we are to spend in company with part of our society) with Mrs. and Miss F. and a brother aide-de-camp, leaving us here for England.

November 8th.—Halt at Monai-Majra. Employed myself during the morning in sketching a small temple and taken in the town, one of the many pretty Hindoo pieces of architecture one sees all over the country. In the afternoon several of us started to escort the ladies to their first day's ground, separate from our camp about six miles, leaving them with a very uncertain prospect of again meeting. Their road was the worst I have seen in the country; dry and wet courses of rivers, large plains with nothing but jungle and sand, was the character of the whole of the country I saw—good, I imagine, only for the wild buffalo, black partridge, tiger, and other game.

November 9th.- A long march of fourteen miles to Kurr, a large enclosed town, the capital of a petty chief to whom the land we passed through to-day mostly belongs; and on the followng day again passed through much fine country, which belongs to the Patialah Rajah. The march ending at a fort of his called Nandpoor, which we had been over in our former expedition through this country. Rode in the evening to one or two large and flourishing villages near the camp.

November 11th.—To get ahead of some of the columns marching on Feeroozpoor, the General has determined not to have the usual Sunday halt, and we accordingly marched to Bussee, a considerable town enclosed with mud walls and a wet and dirty ditch.

November 12th.—Another short and pleasant march to Bootghur, a place just across the great road between Loudiana and Kurnaul, and within a mile or two of Sirhind; to which place I rode in the evening with one or two of the ladies of the camp, in the hope of seeing one of the regiments of cavalry raised for Shah Suja's force, which was supposed to be passing in this direction. We did *not* see the cavalry, but we did see plenty of ruins, among which we were nearly lost.

November 13th—Marched to Esroo, a small town and fort eleven miles from yesterday's ground. Found it necessary to shoot a horse of the Generals from her state of busotty—a disease among horses, peculiar, I believe, to India. It is very catching, and, consequently, most dangesous in a stable. It shews itself in a succession of sores, which break out all over the body, more particularly the legs, which are sometimes twice their natural size from its effects.

From Esroo we continued marching through the same kind of country, *via* Malod to Lattala, where we again halted on a Saturday instead of Sunday. Lattala is a considerable walled town.

November 17th and 18th.—Stayed at Lattala the 17th, and on the 18th marched to Busseeau, a long and sandy road of fifteen miles.

Near our camp we found a large collection of handsome tents—those of a Rajah Adeyne Sing, a native of some rank living in the directi n of Kurnaul.

November 19th.—Another long march of sixteen miles to Wuduee, a place in Shere Sing's territories; a small vilage with a kind of castle of his attached. When we passed through this place in 1837, Shere Sing's mother was shut up in the fort; but since then she is either dead or otherwise disposed of.

November 20th.—Marched to Bagha Purana through a somewhat desolate-looking country which has been the case with our three or four last marches. Sir W. Cotton, the majore-general commanding the first division of the army of the Indus, joined the camp, to remain a day or two with the General and on the 23rd moved on to Feerozepoor; but found after we got in, that to-day is but a temporary encampment, and that we shall have to take up our intended ground in the lines to-morrow morning.

For some time previously Lord Auckland had wished to meet Runjeet Sing on some part of our frontier, and the present period, when chief would be able to see the force intended for the expedition to Affghanistan, was considered as a favourable opportunity. Feeroozpoor, a small town and territory which had lately lapsed to us, was fixed upon for the point of assembly for the different divisons of the army, both as being on the Sutlej (on which river a considerale portion of the army stores had to be forwarded), and as being the frontier town between our own dominions and those of Lahore, and being thus conveniently situated for Runjeet Sing. Some of the regiments had to come from Alahabad on the Ganges, 900 miles off, in addition to the contemplated march onwards ; so that by the time they arrived at Feeroozpoor they had been already on the move for more than two months before.

November 24th.—Changed ground to the other side of Feerozpooor, to be on the extreme right of the lion of troops. The ground we came upon is but indifferent; though not worse than the remaindeɹ of the encamping ground. Rode, after our arrival on the ground, down to the bridge of boats which has lately been built across the Sutlej river, for the convenience of the different interviews between Runjeet Sing and the Governor-general. The part of the river it crosses is narrow, probably not more than 70 or 80 yards ; and the water, of course, from running in so confined a space, flows through it like a mill-sluice. There are about 140 boats collected for the use of army, and one very fine bodgerow ; and two boats for use of the Sir Henry and staff. should he prefer a voyage to travelling with the troops. The high grass jungle, which covers the river bank and both sides, prevents the possibility of any of the tents being pitched nearer the bank than two miles.

November 26th.—Thre brigades, the first, second, and fourth, marched into camp this morning under the command of Sir W. Cotton, part taking up ground to our right, and the remainder to our extreme left. In the evening, the General looked at part of the line in his ride.

November 27th.—The General and all his staff mounted soon after daylight, and rode nearly to the town, where he remained till the Governor-general arrived, and escorted him back to his tents, pitched within about two miles of our own; after which we rode quietly home.

November 28th.—The cavalry and camel-battery of the artillery part of the force came in this morning. The General rode out to meet them, but finding them late did not wait; and after his departure I rode to their lines, met them, and rode in with them. They and their horses looked particularly well, and ready for the long and weary march before them. In the evening we inspected part of the line, and afterwards dined at a large party at the Governor-general's.

November 29th.—To-day being that fixed upon for the first meeting between the Maha Rajah and Governor-general, Sir Henry got into his carriage at daylight, and with three of us proceeded to the great man's camp, in order to be present at the meeting. On arriving there, we found the main street of his camp lined with troops—four regiments of infantry, and portions of two of cavalry, together with a troop and company of artillery, being drawn up. The latter is that which has been lately organised as an experiment, with camels, and which hitherto has more than expectations formed of them. The Chief went into the Governor-general's tent, and having remained there a short time, mounted his horse and inspected the lime drawn up. All the regiments seemed in the best possible order, particularly the Queen's 3rd Buffs.

After waiting some two hours, the Maha Rajah's suwarree was reported to be seen in the distance; upon which the Governor-general mounted his elephant, and, accompanied by the General and all his staff, proceeded to the bottom of the line of troops to meet him. The crowd was what one might expect from the meeting of up-wards of one hundred elephants within the space of as many yards wide, and the crush of course awful; elephants trumpeting, gentlement swearing, and each one trying how he could best poke out his neighbour's eye with the corner of his howdah : while the confusion was not a little heightened by the cannot firing within three yards of one, and frightening our elephants.

But all this was a mere trifle to what was to come. At the entrance of the Governor-general's tent, where all dismounted, the scene of confusion and riot was what I never before saw in India or elsewhere. In consequence of no good or proper arrangement having been mгde, every one, whether belonging to the suite of the Governor-general or the Commander-in-chief, or not, and also those of the Maha Rajha, and upwards of two hundred army officers, all anxious to see the durbar, croweded in tugether, əach pushing, hustling, and elbowing his neighbonr, till at last it was found necessary to bring in two companies of Europeans, and clear a street for the passage of those entitled to sit in the durbar This was at last effected, though not without defficulty, and the select few found their appointed places.

I being one of these, stationed myself behind the General's chair, where I remained the whole of the durbar. It was, as usual with Runjeet, somewhat long, from his having so many question to ask ; but after some three-quarters of an hour he got up and proceeded to examine the presents. These, as usual, consisted of gunг, pistols, swords,and kingcobs. After looking at these for some time, and putting his solitary eye as close as possible to each article, he walked in to the next tent to exnmine two beautiful nine-pound howitzers, both in reality, and in his estimation, the most valuable part of the gifts : they were barss nine-pounders, beautifully inlaid and carved, with a medallion of his own head in the centre of the barrel. These were given him with harness and every thing, even to the most minute articles, complete and ready for service, with one hundred sharp-nel shell. They also gave the old gentleman a very good oil-painting of her Majesty Queen Victoria ; upon the giving of which a royal salute of one hundred guns was fired in honour of it. I do not think he quite understood it, but seemed to think her Majesty made a very decent Nautch girl. After a very long stay he departed under a royal salute, and we marched home with all convenient speed. Something of the same kind was presented to him by Lord W. Bentinck (two iron nine-pounders, I believe which first led to the idea of giving the present guns ; in fact, it is now getting defficult to offer any thing which is new to him, for among the numbers of presents he has had from different Europeans, almost every kind of manufacture has been included—clocks and watches without end, guns enough to furnish all the crack shooters of England, horses and carriages not a few, and, in short, guns are the only things which he will uow be certain to appreciate.